HUNTING
RETRIEVERS

HUNTING RETRIEVERS

Hindsights, Foresights and Insights

James B. Spencer

Alpine Publications Inc.
2456 E. 9th St., Loveland, CO 80537

ISBN 0-931866-40-5

Cover photos: *top left,* Nova Scotia Duck Tolling Retriever, photographed by Arline MacDonald; *top right,* Bill Wheeler and his Golden Retriever, Sonny; *bottom right,* Curly Coated Retriever Ch. Dynamites Anxious Arrival CDX, Cott/Francis photo; *bottom left,* Quartermoon Dixie Lilly SH WCX, Golden Retriever photographed by Bobbie Christensen.

To
My Wife, Theresa

She is a people-person, an indoor type. Still, she has supported my deep need to work with dogs in the outdoors through our thirty-four years together, although she will never understand it. If any of her friends question my sanity— as I'm sure they must—I have no doubt she resolutely swears that "Everyone's out of step but Jim."

Her theory is that men and women are so different that they are two separate species. Thus, it is more important that we accommodate rather than understand one another. That has worked for us. We enjoy each other more now than we did when we were engaged. Viva La Difference!

TABLE OF CONTENTS

PREFACE

This preface contains lies—deliberate, major, stemwinding prevarications, included for the sole purpose of misleading those few citizens who read prefaces.

Perhaps guilt should be welling up within me as I prepare to commit these planned untruths to the permanence of a book preface, where (I fondly hope) they will haunt me for the rest of my life. However, a preface is a combination boudoir and rumpus-room where writers and reviewers interact, so what could be unfair?

In fact, the only people a writer can depend on to read his cherished preface are reviewers. Most other readers push on immediately to the major topics of the opus. They have little time to struggle through the author's meandering afterthoughts about his creation. They don't care that he sits there as bone-weary as if he had painted a barn in a windstorm. They are indifferent to his assessment of the book's position in its genre. They have no interest in a litany of the names of those patron saints and angels "without whom . . . ." No, readers—real live, book-buying readers—want to immerse themselves immediately with the wonderous material that begins in Chapter 1.

Reviewers, however, always read prefaces. Having reviewed many books for several periodicals, I understand why: Prefaces tell the perceptive reader a lot about the book, the author's opinion of the book, and perhaps about the author, too. Because it is the last thing the weary, glassy-eyed scribe commits to paper, and the first thing the fresh, analytical reviewer peruses, the advantage falls to the latter.

In the preface of my earlier book, *Retriever Training Tests,* I committed the folly of being too honest, too modest. Although I had included a large amount of training and handling instruction in every chapter of the book (mostly techniques which had never before appeared in print), I didn't mention that fact in the preface. Even worse, I stated that the book was not a "complete training manual."

I did this for several reasons. First, thinking at the time that everyone read prefaces, I felt obligated to forewarn the paying customers that the book didn't contain a complete, step-by-step training procedure. Second, I wanted to focus the readers' attention on the major purpose of the book, namely to help retriever trainers to set up tests that would accomplish their training goals. And third, I must admit to a bit of false modesty. It seemed to me that if I, after writing in a wealth of original training material, were to humbly take a seat at the foot of the table, the more discerning reviewers would smile on me and say, "Friend, move up higher!"

It didn't work. They took me at my preface word. Reviewer after reviewer—although generally glowing in their benevolence toward my book—either ignored the question of training material or repeated (almost like the surgeon general's warning on cigarette packages) that this book was not a training manual, leaving out the all important word "complete." Not one review mentioned the generous garnish of fresh training techniques I had sprinkled throughout the seven-course meal of tests.

This time things will be different. Though it will be a struggle, I will not allow my native reticence to induce me to downplay the significance of this opus. Here, then, in capsule form is my general assessment:

"This book tells anyone interested in hunting retrievers everything he/she could ever hope to know. Reading it is like receiving infused knowledge from the Diety. Regular readers of Jim Spencer's magazine columns and articles, around which this book is built, say, "Retrievers have ceased to be a problem." Many have noticed substantial improvement in their wing shooting. They catch more and bigger fish. They receive promotions at work. They achieve their optimal weight. Their children behave. Their marriages bubble with romance and passion."

So much for generalities. Now, let me tell you how I have structured this tome to achieve all these wonders in the lives of my readers.

The book you hold contains a collection of my magazine columns and articles about retrievers. Almost every chapter is an adaptation of one, two, or three such pieces. However, not one appears here exactly as it was originally published. Each has been adapted to satisfy the "Unity, Coherence, and Emphasis" needs of this book. (Wouldn't the Jesuits who struggled years ago to instruct me in those three essentials be proud to read that last sentence!)

This appropriately unified, cohering, and emphasized collection of my thoughts *addresses the needs of the first-time hunting retriever buyer.* It tells him what a hunting retriever is and what one can do for him. It describes each of the eight retriever breeds from the hunter's viewpoint in considerable detail. It helps him decide whether he should proceed, or whether he would be better off without a retriever. It tells him how to select the hunting retriever—trained dog or puppy—that has the highest probability of pleasing him. And it tells him how to house his dog. It goes on to tell him about the off-season activities he may want to participate in and the clubs he may want to join. This is everything he/she needs to know before his retriever (puppy or trained dog) moves in and establishes residence. (Being a pre-purchase text, it says not one whit about training. That will be the subject of my next book.)

Section I, "The Hunting Retriever's Job," discusses *the work one can expect from the "ideal" hunting retriever.* Not the "perfect" hunting retriever—with which I have no familiarity—but the "ideal" one as found in the real world. If I seem a bit too forgiving of certain imperfections, it is because I have had extensive practice in forgiving them in my many lovably "ideal" retrievers. Even in areas where my own dogs have generally excelled, like nose, I express my suspicion that I could have made do with much less. I end Section I with the story of Duffy, my Golden that lived here for over sixteen years, certainly a dog with faults, but one I would take back for another sixteen if I only could.

In Section II, "The Eight Retriever Breeds," I present a hunter's *profile of each breed.* Unlike breed books, which concentrate on breed development and history because they are written by and for addicts, these chapters address the hunter who knows little of the breed, the hunter who would first like to understand the hunting characteristics before delving into the seeming fantasyland of breed history. Thus these chapters *emphasize personality, temperament, trainability, maturity rate, and physical make-up.* Underlying these descriptions is my personal feeling that traits are neither good nor bad in themselves; the owner's attitude makes them so. One person may be delighted with a hyperactive retriever, while another may tire just watching so much energy. One person may enjoy combing and brushing a long coat, while another may despise such work. One person may want a retriever that can do light-duty as a watchdog on the side, while another may prefer a dog that is everybody's friend. And so on. Thus, I have not tried to sort each breed's traits into an arbitrary list of good-uns and bad-uns. That would only be my interpretation, made from my personal knothole. Instead, I simply describe a typical dog of each breed, trying to present a three-dimensional model from which the hunter can judge the breed according to his personal likes and dislikes. To minimize my personal prejudices, I have reached beyond my own observations and experience for material. For every breed—including those I have been training, hunting, feeding, and cleaning up after for decades—I have sought input from respected breeders and trainers; people who know and love each breed.

In **Section III, "Acquiring Your Hunting Retriever,"** I *help the reader decide whether he/she should buy a retriever* or whether some other option better suits his/her needs. Then, I explain the two general choices for those who decide on a retriever: the trained dog, and the puppy, pointing out the cost/risk trade-offs involved. Finally, I discuss proper housing for the hunting retriever, and offer what may be a surprising suggestion to the one-dog owner.

In **Section IV, "The Hunting Retriever Owner's World,"** I present *information about the various off-season activities available* today to the owner of a hunting retriever and about the clubs and organizations he may wish to join. We have had highly competitive (and correspondingly expensive) AKC-licensed field trials since the 1930s. While probably less than 10 percent of retriever owners can afford to play this game, everyone should understand how it works and what it has always contributed to the breeds. Ditto for the working certificate tests which have been offered by the various national breed clubs for decades, primarily for dog show people interested in demonstrating that their stock can do basic field work. I give extensive coverage—both an explanation and an evaluation—to the new hunting retriever tests which have introduced significant new options to the middle-class retrieverite, filling the gap between traditional field trials and working certificate tests.

In Section IV I also explain all the *clubs* the neophyte retriever owner has so much difficulty finding out about: national breed clubs, local breed clubs, field trial clubs, hunting test clubs, obedience training clubs, and local kennel clubs.

In Appendix I, I have put together a glossary of hunting retriever terms I would love to have had when I started out. In Appendix II, I have listed the names and addresses of important contacts, and appropriate magazines.

Acknowledgements

As I mentioned, I sought input from many retriever experts in each breed before writing the columns and articles around which this book is based. Any list I might make up now may be seriously incomplete, but still I feel that I should express my appreciation to as many of them as I can recall. Here goes:

LABRADOR RETRIEVERS:
Maryanne Foote, Helen Ginnel, D.L. Walters.

GOLDEN RETRIEVERS:
Simpson Bowles, Nick Hammond,
and all the many other members of GRCA I have visited
with over the years at trials, tests, shows, obedience
trials, and GRCA national specialties.

CHESAPEAKE BAY RETRIEVERS:
Nancy Lowenthal, Jane Pappler, Emelise Baughman.

FLAT-COATED RETRIEVERS:
Bunny Milikin, Sally Terroux, Gloria Mundell.

CURLY-COATED RETRIEVERS:
Dick Guerin, Kathy Tucker, Janean Marti,
Debbie Wales, Mike & Sue Tokolics.

IRISH WATER SPANIELS:
Elissa Kirkegard, Pat Brenner, Ted Brenner

AMERICAN WATER SPANIELS:
Tom Olson, Vaughn Brockman, Gary Forshee,
Sharon Beaupre, Doug Doyle.

NOVA SCOTIA DUCK TOLLING RETRIEVER:
Sylvia VanSloun, John Richardson, Alison Strang,
Arline MacDonald, Dennis Robbins, Avery Nickerson.

SECTION I:

THE HUNTING RETRIEVER'S JOB

When a person sets about to explain what any type of hunting dog does for a living, he can easily overdo it and describe a pinnacle of perfection that no dog ever has or ever will achieve. Perhaps the more dogs he has seen, the more difficulty a person has being realistic. Each "good" working dog excels at certain things, skims by at others, and fails at a few. Memory is kind. We forget that the dog with, say, outstanding marking ability was too independent to be "handled" easily to blind retrieves.

Conversely, the dog that was always a delight to handle to blind retrieves probably didn't mark very well, thereby often requiring help from the boss on retrieves he should have done on his own. And, the dog that possessed slash and dash aplenty may well have been just a tad rough on birds, not hardmouthed you understand, but, well, you know. It's so tempting to combine the only virtues of many dogs into a single description, leaving out all of their faults.

However, that just isn't reality as the owners of hunting retrievers experience it. Thus, in Chapter 1, where I describe the "ideal" retriever, I definitely do not write of the perfect retriever. Maybe I have only set down "minimum requirements" lest my delightful memories of many retrievers induce me to describe an animal I have never seen under a single coat.

If your retriever-owning friends tell you that their dogs far surpass my description of the ideal retriever, good for them. I wear rosy glasses for most of my dogs, too. We're all a little like the golfer who, no matter how dismal his score may be for a given round, will entertain himself for hours telling anyone who will listen about the two or three good shots he hit that day. Climb up on the bar stool next to me at a retriever party and I will entertain myself similarly by telling you about my dogs—all of them if I really get you cornered.

In Chapter 2, I recount the highlights of the very long life of one "ideal" (not perfect) retriever, my old Duffy. He did a lot more for me than pick up game birds. He did a lot for the whole family, and you need to understand that side of owning a hunting retriever, too.

He died, after sixteen and a half years. That is a long life for a dog, but it wasn't long enough. I still miss him in the duckblind, in the uplands, in the backyard, by my chair. You need to understand that about hunting retrievers, too. They are much farther from immortal than we are. If you own one, you will mourn one.

Yet, the memories of Duffy outweigh the pain of his absence, and I have found a little of Duffy in his successors: a facial expression, a movement, a fault. All help me bond with these youngsters.

Mickey could do the work, but he wasn't my kind of dog.

1

THE IDEAL HUNTING RETRIEVER

Everyone think like me, everyone want my squaw,'' said a wise old Indian who certainly deserves the envy of both Confusius and Shakespeare. Fortunately, we don't think alike—about squaws, shotguns, decoys, calls, and, perhaps especially, about retrievers. I've seen several highly competent water dogs that I personally could not enjoy sharing a blind and a sandwich with. Understand: I am not talking about worthless mutts that no one could train to pick up hamburger off the kitchen floor. I am talking about well-bred, well-trained retrievers that I simply couldn't enjoy working with.

Take Mickey, for example. Many years ago two of my kids and I trained three littermate Golden Retrievers. I owned the dam, and selected the sire of this litter with as much care as parents of another era chose husbands for their daughters. All six pups turned out well, lending my judgement of breeding stock more merit than some of my other selections would support. After the kids selected their pups, I chose Mickey as the best of what was left. The three of us spent over two years on the project, and from a parent's point of view it was a delightful time. However, Mickey and I just weren't made for each other. Sure, he had plenty of good qualities: loved to retrieve, loved water, loved birds (which is not always synonomous with loving to retrieve), and was eager (almost over-anxious) to please. He did very well in the puppy and derby stakes at our local retriever club's fun trials. On top of all that, he was lovable as a pet. Sounds ideal, doesn't he?

Well, he was ideal—at least for the people I placed him with after I had had all I could take. They loved him and found him to be the best hunting dog they had ever had. In fact, when he died, they called me to ask if by chance I had another ''washout'' they could buy.

For me, however, he just wasn't right. He lacked the sparkle and dash that means so much to me. He could do the job all right, but I couldn't really enjoy watching him do it; his work never once made the hackles on my neck tingle. Then, too, unlike most Goldens, he was not overly bright. While he was anxious to please, he didn't learn quickly, and even after he grasped something, it took drill, drill, and more drill to tatoo the lesson on his clouded mind. Slow, grinding work, with lots of going back to square one interspersed among periods of painstaking progress. Nature didn't design me for a canine lifetime of that, so once I had drilled the basics into him, I placed him with the family of hunters mentioned above. That was a good move for all of us, especially for Mickey, for he coasted comfortably the rest of his life on what I had taught him—no more struggles to learn something new.

I once knew a professional retriever trainer who would have loved Mickey. He told me, ''I want them just smart enough to pick up the bird. I'll teach them everything else. Trouble with smart dogs is they are always thinking up new ways to stick it to a guy. Give me the dumb ones every time.''

Duffy, on the other hand, was my kind of dog from the first. When I saw him as a seven-week-old pup, he was fast and stylish, quick to learn, eager to please, and from the start neither of us had any problem overlooking each other's faults—and we both had serious ones. He was a mediocre marker even on his good days, so I frequently had to handle him (with whistle and arm signals) to birds he should have found on his own. This limited his field trial success, but I couldn't bring myself to let even that upset me. For his part, he overlooked my poor shooting and occasional fits of temper all his life. Duffy died in 1984 at the age of sixteen and a half, but two of his pictures will hang in my den near my gun rack as long as I live. I hope each of you someday has a retriever that delights you for as many years as Duffy has delighted me, first in life and now in memory.

(Adapted from ''The 'Ideal' Retriever,'' *Wildfowl*, August/September, 1985.)

The point I would like to make here is that the "ideal" retriever is not a perfect retriever anymore than the less-than-ideal retriever is worthless. "Ideal" is very personal, very subjective. For someone else, Duffy would have been a washout, just as Mickey turned out to be a treasure in life and in death.

The "ideal" retriever for you is the one you truly enjoy working and hunting with, the one whose virtues stimulate you, the one whose faults disturb you only slightly. The "ideal" retriever for you is the retriever with which you can establish and maintain strong rapport.

The rapport level dominates every human/canine relationship. Where it binds, "God's in His Heaven and all's right with the world." Where it divides, divorce is inevitable—and the sooner the better for both. There are countless human temperaments and countless canine temperaments. The trick is to properly match them.

Breed preference constitutes one important dimension of rapport. There are many breeds to choose from. First, there are the six AKC-recognized retriever breeds: Labrador, Golden, Chesapeake Bay, Flat-Coated, Curly-Coated, and Irish Water Spaniel. Then, there is the American Water Spaniel, an AKC-recognized breed that has never been classified as either a retriever or a spaniel. The nifty little Canadian, the Nova Scotia Duck Tolling Retriever, has been recently recognized by the United Kennel Club (UKC), but has not yet received AKC's blessing. Neither that fact nor the breed's confusing resume-like name prevents the Toller from doing outstanding work as a retriever. Thus, there are actually eight "retriever" breeds to choose from. Some will wonder that I am not including the various spaniel and pointing breeds, since most of them retrieve. However, here we are discussing only the breeds built to endure the fierce

A retriever should retrieve upland game birds, as 'Bud', a yellow Lab, does for owner Randy Case.

winds and icy waves the duck dog must withstand to fulfill the "ideal" retriever's job description.

Sex is another important aspect of rapport—and nothing else. Some people enjoy working with males; others with females. If you go with your gut here, you will be happy. If you follow someone else's "profoundly logical" reasons for selecting the sex opposite of what you really want, you will be unhappy.

Within your choice of breed and sex, there are individuals you can fall in love with, individuals that you could never give a damn about one way or the other, and individuals you could cordially hate at best. Finding the right dog within your chosen breed is the subject of another section in this book. Here let it suffice to say that both breed and individual dog are important to the kind of rapport you should have with your "ideal" retriever.

Granting that rapport, which is highly subjective and personal, constitutes the most important single factor in the "ideal" retriever, we must acknowledge that it is not the only factor. The animal must be more than a lovable canine soul mate. He must perform meaningful labor for you: in the duckblind, in the goose pit, in the uplands. To succeed in his occupational mission in life, a retriever must possess a combination of natural instincts and training. Let me explain.

To visualize the unique position of retrievers in the world of hunting dogs, picture a continuum, or line of increasing values of one trait and decreasing values of another. Place "100 percent natural ability" at the left end and "100 percent training" at the right. As you proceed from left to right along this line, natural ability decreases and training increases. The various classes of dogs fall somewhere along that continuum, depending on the mixture of breeding and training required to bring out their best.

Hounds, for example, occupy a spot not far from the extreme left, because little training, but much natural ability is required in a good hound. Once at a sight hound lure coursing competition, I asked one of the owners how one goes about training a dog to chase the little patch of fur. He looked puzzled, and finally said, "You don't. They just do it."

Big running pointers and setters fall a little farther to the right, still depending heavily on natural abilities but needing a modicum of training (staunching, steadying, minimal obedience). Failure to understand this underlies the many complaints from the inexperienced about the difficulty they have controlling a pointer or setter. They want more control than the dogs can give them.

The continental pointing breeds are still farther to the right, requiring a bit more training (retrieving, more restricted range, greater obedience). These are nice, upland game pointing dogs just as they came from the old country—close-working, obedient, outstanding noses, natural retrievers—if we can just keep them that way.

However, too many field trialers seem intent on making pointers and setters of them.

Flushing spaniels occupy the center of the continuum, needing an approximately equal mixture of natural abilities and training. The flusher must hunt with a lot of hustle, put his birds in the air promptly, and retrieve naturally. However, he must be trained to stay within gun range, to stop after the flush (so the boss can shoot), and to do all the basic obedience exercises.

Retrievers fall quite far to the right, requiring more training than natural abilities. Just as hounds are more born than made, retrievers are more made than born. Please understand: Breeding contributes significantly to the ideal retriever; however, training contributes substantially more. A retriever must master more learned behavior before he can be called "finished" than must any other type of hunting dog. The retriever must learn more control, more commands, more responses, more sustained responses, and more complex responses.

Nevertheless, natural abilities, acquired through the genes, contribute significantly to the make-up of the ideal retriever. If the animal lacks the "insides" of a working retriever, even the most talented trainer will not make much of him. On the other hand, a dog with the right instincts will make his trainer, whether a pro or stumbling beginner, look better than he deserves.

So, what are the natural abilities a good retriever should possess as standard equipment?

"Desire"—and all the word connotes in hunting retriever language—is *sine qua non* (without which there is nothing). If the beast cares little for birds, finds retrieving a bore, or disdains water, you shouldn't waste your time trying to train him. I once tossed away two years on a Lab bitch that had an impeccable pedigree but only now-and-then desire. She would really work for me about one day in three. On the other two, her attitude varied from nonchalant to resentful. When she did well, I dreamed of national championships, but most of the time I spent the late evening studying her pedigree, assuring myself that a dog with such sterling ancestors just had to come around. She never changed. Two years I spent on that aristocratic mutt. I hope my experience with her will convince you not to be so stubborn. Don't try to fill an inside straight with a dog that lacks that all-important "gut card," desire, especially when the stakes are years from your own life, years you only spend once.

Besides desire, there are a couple of other natural abilities of some importance: nose, and marking.

My thoughts on "nose" may at first impress you as heretical, but they do explain why scenting ability is seldom mentioned in knowledgeable retriever circles. "Nose" means less to a retriever than to the other hunting dogs. Our American preoccupation with the magic of the canine proboscis comes from the worlds of scent hounds and pointing breeds. Hounds with "cold noses" can locate

A retriever should be able to mark in water with lots of cover.

and follow trails that lesser floppy-eared crooners would bypass. Similarly, a bird dog with discriminating nostrils will pick up a distant whiff of bird that a lesser dog would miss. However, nothing like this exists in the retriever's work-a-day world. His primary job is marking and picking up birds that have been shot. If the retriever has marked a fall well, he needs only an average canine nose (no better than that of, say, Spitz or Great Dane), to scent the bird within the area of the fall, or to trail it if it is a runner. Even in hunting to the gun in the uplands, in which the retriever does locate and flush birds, an average nose will locate any bird in his immediate vicinity. Since the dog must stay within open-bore shotgun range of the hunter, rather than range wide like a pointing dog, few birds will escape the notice of a very ordinary snout.

Don't misunderstand: I like to see a retriever with an outstanding nose, a dog that "hooks" (winds) his birds from a considerable distance. However, the minimum scenting requirements for retrievers just aren't all that demanding. In the hundreds, maybe thousands, of retrievers I have seen over the past thirty years, I have only seen one with a nose that made me suspicious. I judged this animal twice in hunting retriever tests and she had more difficulty finding her marks than any of the other dogs entered: seemed to run right over a bird a couple of times. However, she was not consistently bad, so on neither occasion could my co-judge and I convince ourselves that her problems were solely due to inadequate scenting power.

Besides a reasonable nose, the ideal retriever should possess enough "marking" ability to assure you that he will pick up most of the birds you down. As a group, retrievers excel in marking when compared to the pointing and spaniel breeds. However, within the retriever group, there are many degrees of marking ability, and different owners expect different levels of proficiency. Personally, I have never owned an outstanding marker by field trial standards: a dog that "pins" or "steps on" every bird. However, I have seen (and greatly admired) many of them. Most of my better retrievers have been either hunting fools (dogs that stayed out there and hunted like a spaniel until they found the bird), or good handling dogs, like Duffy, that relied on whistle and arm signals more than they should have. So you see, there is some latitude in marking ability among "ideal" retrievers. The important thing to remember is that the trait is inherited, so what you buy is all you will ever have. You can't train your retriever to mark better than his genes allow.

Besides rapport with the boss and natural ability, the "ideal" retriever needs copious quantities of *training*, the first level of which is basic obedience. The animal must be taught to respond to the basic commands: KENNEL, RELEASE, SIT, DOWN, STAY, HEEL, and COME-IN, which distinguish a canine companion from a pain in the bar-stool region. A retriever must be under control most of the time during a hunt or he will ruin everything for everybody.

He should HEEL to and from the blind, to avoid difficulties with other dogs in the area and to make transporting of decoys and other equipment as hazardless as possible for the boss and others who share the boss's blind. He should remain quietly on a SIT or DOWN and STAY, in or near the blind (or any other convenient place), without moving, barking, whining, or breaking, so that decoying birds will not think better of their decision to join all those delightful ducks sitting so happily there below them.

A well-trained retriever should heel obediently.

In the uplands, the retriever must SIT on whistle or voice command whenever he reaches the limits of his boss's shotgun range—even when he has fresh, running pheasant scent in his nostrils. After all, the object of the game is to shoot the bird, not just to put it in the air as quickly as possible. Similarly, the retriever should COME-IN on whistle or voice command when he reaches the extremes of his range to the boss's left or right and clearly has not struck bird scent. That makes him a close-working dog that hunts objectives, but doesn't necessarily do windshield-wiper quartering.

The next level of training consists of combining control with natural abilities. The dog should be steady, should mark and remember at least two falls from the same flock, should deliver to hand, and should be familiar with the various accouterments of hunting: boats, calls, blinds, guns. He should disdain interaction with decoys, and heed the gospel relative to bank-running.

The final, most demanding, and most enjoyable level of training consists of mastering the blind retrieve. This exercise is one in which the dog has not seen a bird fall, but is directed to it by the handler through whistle and arm signals. Many hunting situations require this set of skills. For example, while hunting ducks over decoys, a person might shoot a couple of mallards, one falling within spitting distance and the other flapping and sailing 150 to 200 yards before hitting the ground across the pond. The dog would surely see the duck that fell right in the decoys, but may have missed the other fall, especially if several ducks flew away unharmed.

When the retriever drops the first duck in the hunter's outstretched mitt, he has no idea that he has more work to do. However, if he has been trained on blind retrieves, his proud owner simply needs to sit him facing the other fall and say, "Dead bird . . . Line . . . Back," and the dog will start swimming toward the unseen bird. If he drifts off-line as he goes, the owner has only to blow a sharp whistle blast to get his attention and then give him an appropriate arm signal to redirect him. It's like hunting with a guided missile, as James Lamb Free said in his 1949 classic *Training Your Retriever*.

There are three parts to the blind retrieve: lining, which is sending the dog on his initial "line" to the bird; stopping, which is getting the dog to turn and look at you for an arm or whistle signal; and casting, which is redirecting the dog with an arm or whistle signal after he has been stopped.

An air of mystery surrounds the blind retrieve in the minds of many beginners, and some long-time retriever owners as well. The same aura surrounds fly casting for many novice fishermen. Yet, I started all five of my kids with fly rods before they entered kindergarten, and none of them had any difficulty with the basics. Of course, there are artists with the fly rod who can make their slim wands do magic, but that level of proficiency wasn't necessary for my kids to catch panfish on popper bugs. Ditto for the blind retrieve. It ranges from very basic to "oh-my-God," and each owner can choose the level his own dog should achieve to be "ideal."

Anyone who can teach a dog to HEEL can teach him all three of the blind retrieve skills well enough to "catch panfish with popper bugs." Further, he can spend the rest of his dog's life teaching him more and more advanced blind retrieves; just as the fly fisherman can learn more advanced casts, and never master them all. Most important for the beginner, however, is the fact that he can get by nicely—pick up 80 percent of the birds he is now losing because his dog doesn't see them—with just the rudiments of blind retrieve training.

So, there is the "ideal" retriever: a dog of your chosen breed and sex, a dog with which you have rapport, a dog with adequate natural instincts, and a dog with considerable training.

A retriever should mark and remember two falls from the same flock, as Beaver did here for Pat Spencer.

The dog should sit quietly by the blind.

2
DUFFY
Duncan Dell's MacDuff C.D. 2/7/68 - 8/14/84

"Good-bye, old timer," was trite, but it was all I could muster as I gently patted Duffy's ancient shoulder before my son, Pat, carried him to the truck for his last ride to the vet's. He looked at me, glassy-eyed, with the look of the scourged Jesus.

Only once before had he shown me that expression. He was then two years old, and suffering through my groping blind retrieve training "methodology." I can't remember what went wrong, what it was I couldn't communicate to him—he would do anything I could make him understand—but I went into a rage, out there in the pasture, in front of two of my children. Professional trainer, Dean Campbell once told me that the first two licks with a whip are for the dog; any more than two are for the trainer, showing that he is out of control. How many did I give Duffy that evening? Eight blows? Ten? I don't know how many. I only remember my oldest daughter, Terry, then about fourteen, screaming "Stop! Stop! Daddy, STOP!" I stopped, and I looked at Duffy, and saw the look of the scourged Jesus. Never again, I thought. But I hadn't counted on the last look he would ever give me.

A dog's last day is always a sad one, of course, but down deep I believe that death is only a tragedy for those who have never lived. And Duffy REALLY lived—for sixteen and a half years.

Back in the late 1950s I had helped Sim Bowles train a couple of Golden Retrievers for field work. By 1968, when I decided to buy a Golden of my own, Sim was dead, but his kennel name (Duncan Dell) lived on and Sim's bloodlines were still flowing through Duncan Dell dogs. That is what I had to have, of course, Sim's bloodlines.

There were eleven in the litter, but five people were ahead of me when it came time to select puppies. Only

three males were left when my turn came, but I think Duffy would have been my choice even if I had had the entire litter to choose from. The way he looked at me, the way he frolicked to me when I squatted and clapped my hands, the way he snuggled up against my leg, told me that this was the one with which I had the most rapport. Since there had been some problem with his birth, I named him after MacDuff in Shakespeare's play, *MacBeth,* for "MacDuff was from his mother's womb untimely ripped."

At that time we (my wife Theresa, our five kids, and I) lived where only two dogs were allowed. My oldest daughter, Terry, got a female littermate to Duffy that day, so our quota was full. We later moved to where we could have more dogs, but initially Duffy and littermate, Cindy, had to do it all for us, especially Duffy. He had to be my hunting dog, my field trial dog, my show dog, the kids' junior showmanship dog, and everybody's buddy. He did all that, and threw in some obedience trial work to boot. Thus he became a three-sport letterman: field, conformation, and obedience.

Duffy and I a week after I bought him.

(Adapted from "Duffy, A Dog For All Seasons," *Wildfowl,* April/May, 1988.)

The two stars after his name indicate that he placed in AKC-licensed field trials. His record was not all that imposing, actually, for he only placed in the qualifying stake and never higher than third. Nevertheless, his slash, dash—then quite rare in Goldens—and gorgeous conformation so captivated one rich field trialer that he hounded me for years to sell him Duffy. You know the pitch: "You have all these kids to raise and educate, and I'm offering you a lot of money; besides, who's to say Duffy won't be dead in thirty days? Take the money while you can." He made a real pain of himself, but Duffy lived and died mine, and somehow my wife and I managed to raise and educate our five kids without his "charity," thank you.

Duffy's most memorable field accomplishments, however, were in hunting, not field trials.

I introduced my son, Bob, to "real" hunting (as opposed to walking along while Dad shot the birds) at a farm pond on the opening day of dove season when he was eleven. He carried his new Hunter Safety Card and 20-gauge pump—I never liked the idea of starting a kid with a gun that only shoots once. Duffy, then three and a half, was there; so was my still spectating eight-year-old son, Pat (who would, thirteen years later, take Duffy for his last trip to the vet).

Doves were flying that evening, and I shot a couple for Duffy to retrieve. While he was busy with the second, Bob shot his very first bird. You know how important that first bird is, especially when you are only eleven. You want to touch it, hold it, look for the places where you hit it, smooth its feathers, and just plain possess it.

The bird fell near the edge of a small island in the middle of the pond, where Bob couldn't get to it, so it was up to Duffy. If was a simple blind retrieve, maybe forty or fifty yards, with no hazards. In later years, after being polished by Pro Jim Robinson, Duffy would do much tougher ones in field trials, but no other blind retrieve was as important to me as this one. He made it look as easy as it was: just swam out, took one little "Over" cast and came back with the bird. We celebrated there on the shore, and again at home.

Two years later, it was ten-year-old Pat's turn. While Pat is a natural athlete with excellent coordination, he wanted that first bird so much he choked through dove season and the early duck season. He fretted and became more and more frustrated at his lack of success.

One day when a flock of mallards came in to our stool, all three of us stood up and shot, knocking down two birds. In a rare (for me at least) stroke of parental genius, I awarded one of them to Pat as his "official" first bird, even though none of us was sure who had hit it. That did the trick. Pat lost the grim determination that had kept him from success, and a little later, when a hen mallard flew by at about thirty-five yards, I told Pat to take it. He stood up, swung through, and nailed her with one pull of the trigger. Duffy saw the fall, and I sent him

into the choppy water of the large impoundment on which we were hunting. When Duffy approached, the susie came to life and went under. Duffy dove too. Up and down went the bird and the dog, as we stood by helplessly. It took awhile but Duffy hung in there with the lively cripple and finally wrapped his big maw around her.

As I handed Pat the bird, I said, "This is *really* your first bird, Pat. No one else shot at it." Pat grinned a ten-year-old's grin at me—and then out-shot me the rest of the day. He still shows me no mercy today.

Duffy's dog show career was patchy but quite successful. Even with my inept handling, he won several championship points in very limited showing, and once went Best-of-Breed over one of the all-time great show Goldens. Mostly he tolerated dog shows, although he exhibited dignified patience as one Spencer kid after another led him around the ring in junior showmanship. Strong enough to pull any two of them, he was always the gentleman and obeyed the little tugs on his collar from even my smallest daughter, Sheila.

At one point he unwittingly contributed to the myth that show dogs are worthless in the field. That occurred when the Big-Time Outdoor Writer (hereafter referred to as BTOW) graced a show with his presence. First, a little background information: In shows, dogs are judged on how well they conform to the written breed standard of physical perfection; hence the name "conformation."

Whoever says that good hunting dogs can't be pets has never had a Duffy. Here my daughter Sally grooms him.

on how well they conform to the written breed standard of physical perfection; hence the name "conformation."

The Spencer clan showed four dogs that day: Duffy, who by then had licensed qualifying placements as well as several years of actual hunting; and three young Goldens that we also ran quite successfully in the derby stake at field trials. At noon, we went to lunch in shifts so there would always be at least one family member present where our dogs were crated. When I returned from lunch, Bob mentioned that BTOW had come by while I was gone.

"Did he ask whether these dogs were hunted or trialed?" I asked.

"Naw. He just took pictures and stuff."

"Well, did you tell him anyhow?"

"Naw."

"Why not, for God's sake. He needs to know things like that."

"Couldn't. He was too busy making sure everyone knew who he was."

Not long after that, BTOW's column consisted of a diatribe against dog shows as the source of all hunting dog problems in the world today. However, he used the word *confirmation* (which is a sacrament that to my knowledge has never been administered at a dog show), rather than *conformation*. He used the word *confirma-*

tion at least thirty times, blaming it for all the evils that have befallen mankind since Adam and Eve shared an ill-advised apple, thereby exposing his inexcusable ignorance of what he witnessed that day. I thought about writing a letter to the editor requesting that the man at least be taught how to spell the word, even though there was little hope that he would ever understand it. Maybe I should have, but it was autumn and I had better things to do, like hunt our worthless show dogs.

So much for Duffy's contribution to canine myth and unfounded legends. Duffy's third sport was AKC obedience trials, where he quickly acquired the title "Companion Dog" (indicated by the "CD" after his name) with good scores when he was five. To win this title the dog must qualify in three different trials (each qualification is called a "leg") with a score of at least 170 out of a possible 200 points. If a dog earns the title in his first three trials with all scores of 195 or better, he wins the "Dog World Award of Canine Distinction," which is quite an accomplishment in obedience trial circles.

Duffy made scores of 196 and 198 in his first outings, and I thought the Dog World Award was in the bag. However, I overextended him a bit in his third leg which took place in the 1973 Golden Retriever Club of America's national specialty in Mundelein, Illinois. I entered him in all three activities: field trial, conforma-

Duffy was a 3-sport letterman, with significant accomplishments in field trials, conformation, and obedience trials.

9

tion, and obedience. On Friday and Saturday he "JAM'ed" (received a "Judges' Award of Merit") in the qualifying stake of the field trial, but got his coat full of mud, seaweed, and related gunk. I had to bathe him that evening for the conformation show on Sunday. The bath left him so fluffy that he looked twenty pounds heavier than he actually was, so he did not get a serious look in conformation. Immediately after prancing him around the show ring, I had to take him into the obedience ring, where he was so confused by the change from field to bench and bench to obedience that he only scored 190 points. Still that was good enough to complete his CD, and much better than many dogs do on their best days. Besides, he had competed respectably in all three activities at a national specialty, and I was proud of him, Dog World Award or no Dog World Award.

But Duffy was more than a three sport letterman; he was part of the family and patriarch of the kennel for many years after his "careers" were over. He helped us raise several litters, although in later life he lost his enthusiasm for paternal duties. As soon as he saw a pregnant bitch, he would look at me as if to say, "Please, no more of those feisty little things with the sharp teeth." Unlike most male dogs, he never snarled at a pup, no matter how bodacious it became. He simply moved away, sometimes carrying whatever treasure (ball, stick, beer can) the pup was after; at other times he left it there, happy just to escape the puppy's impetuosity.

Even after he was too old to hunt, he would retrieve a dummy in the backyard as often as I would throw it. In his final few years, when he became a housepet, he would bawl and bellow piteously if I tossed a dummy for another dog outside where he could see it through the picture window. For awhile, I responded to his anguish by bringing him out for a retrieve of his own. However, as he got older, it pained me to watch him struggle after it. This animal that had been so flashy, so stylish through his middle years, could now only limp slowly out and back, sometimes stumbling and falling half-way to the ground. Still, making the retrieve was everything to Duffy, and he looked at me with the old passion as he sat painfully to deliver. The fire within was still there, but the physical animal belonged by the fireside, not out in back chasing pointless dummies.

I scratched his chin a lot those last few years as he sat by my chair. He had always liked that. Many times over the years as I sat in a duck blind with Duffy, I called birds with one hand and scratched his chin with the other. Except when there were birds to retrieve, he nuzzled my arm insistently whenever I stopped, or even paused. He did the same in the family room in his old age, only there I had time to observe his pleading look as he shoved my hand up and let it drop.

He constantly followed me around the house, lying down every time I stopped. He watched me all the time, and read when I was about to move again. Each time he raised himself up to follow me, it was a little slower, a little more painful. His face grew white. His once lush coat dried and thinned. His visible ribs and backbone attested to his diminishing interest in food.

"He's over sixteen years old, for God's sake. What are we doing, going for some kind of record?" I asked Theresa, my wife.

"It's your decision. He's your dog. Don't ask me to say when it has to be done. I just couldn't."

"He hurts every time he moves. He slipped and fell in the kitchen again today, and I had to help him back up."

"Please, leave me out of it. I can't. I just can't."

"He's had a good life, Dad," my now twenty-one-year-old son Pat said, "but he's really in pain. You want me to take him to the vet? You don't have to go."

"What I want is for Duffy to be young again . . . to see his tail go up and whip around in circles when he finds a bird . . . to see his truculent way of carrying a beer can . . . to watch him learn to swim again. Most of all, I guess I want him to frolic to me like he did the day I picked him out."

"We all do, Dad; I know, and Mom knows. But should I take him to the vet's now?"

"Yeah, I suppose . . . But I can't go, Pat . . . Too busy today . . . I've got some things to do out in the backyard with the pups . . . The kennel needs cleaning up, too . . . Always a mess this time of day . . . Goodbye, old-timer."

And there it was—the look of the scourged Jesus.

Duffy at 14 years, white-faced and slow, but he lived another 2.5 years.

10

Rumrunner's Brandy and I had strong rapport through his 11 years. (Photo by Jim Reid.)

11

SECTION II:

THE EIGHT RETRIEVER BREEDS

The eight retriever breeds share one unfortunate circumstance with the college football teams in the Big Eight Conference: both consist of "the big two and the little six."

Since I grew up in Nebraska, where folks learn to support the Nebraska University football team before teething, I remember better days for the Conference. Back in the 1930s, when it was the Big Six (sans Colorado and Oklahoma State), several teams now in the "little six" beat up on the "big two" reasonably often. Paul Christman, Missouri's single-wing tailback, filled the stadium with deadly spirals. Elmer Hackney, Kansas State's wild-horse fullback, bucked and churned under the weight of the entire defensive line for five yards a carry. Pete Bausch, Kansas' rough-n-tumble tackle laid waste one offensive backfield after another. In those days Conference championship didn't go automatically to the winner of the Nebraska/Oklahoma fracas.

No such happier days ever existed for the eight retriever breeds. In this country, the Labrador and the Golden have long dominated. True, the Flat-coat was once the top breed in England, but that was long ago. No other breed has achieved the popularity each would seem to deserve, judging from their merits as hunting retrievers.

While I hope that better days await both Big Eight football and the retriever breeds, I have only the vaguest notion of what the "little six" schools need to get back into the game. However, I feel that I know precisely what the "little six" retriever breeds need—exposure. These six breeds can already do the work, as both waterfowl retrievers and upland bird flushers. They indeed do the work every fall for the few dedicated fanciers who use them. The only problem is: Many a hunter who would happily swap a year's duck lease for a dog of one of these breeds doesn't know the breed exists—or at least doesn't know about its unique position within the array of retrievers. The general thinking is that if you need a retriever, you need a Labrador, and if you don't like Labs, you should get a Golden.

For many, that is true. You may be a person who would be best served by a Lab or Golden. If you are, you are fortunate, for good ones are easy to find.

However, before you uncap your pen and open your checkbook, why not take a look at the other retriever breeds?

The following nine chapters describe the eight retriever breeds (two are dedicated to the Labrador). I have tried to show each breed in its entirety—*all* its characteristics, not just those that appeal to me. I feel that no breed characteristic is good or bad in and of itself; the owner's attitude determines its quality. What I like you may well dislike, and vice versa. Thus, I do not present the traits of any breed from the bias of my own knothole. Nor have I limited my material to my own experiences and observations. I have spent many hours conducting telephone interviews with heavy-weight fanciers of each breed (even breeds I have owned for years and those currently in my kennel runs) to get their valuable perspectives. I quote many of them in these chapters.

One hears much these days about breed splits: A single breed having two distinct types, one for field and one for dog shows. Among the retriever breeds, only the Labrador and Golden have gained enough popularity to have experienced this problem, if it is indeed a problem. In chapter 4 I present what I feel is a balanced view of breed splits.

3

THE LABRADOR: EVERYMAN'S RETRIEVER

The Labrador is a stocky, medium-sized dog—about 21- to 25-inches at the withers (top of shoulders) and 55- to 70-pounds, with a short, water-repellent coat that may be black, yellow, or chocolate.

The breed is so widely known today that many people use the name ''Lab'' as a generic term meaning ''retriever.'' For example, in the spring of 1985 right after my son Bob was ordained a priest, a comment was made in the local retriever club's newsletter that Bob would probably get another Lab and get back into retriever training. Indeed, in his junior high days he did train, hunt, and field trial a retriever—did it very well as a matter of fact—but his dog wasn't a Lab. Brandy was a Golden, and I would guess that every dog Pere Robert ever owns will be a Golden. The next time I saw Mark Schreiber, the newsletter editor, I feigned outrage at such a horrible journalistic faux pas. I told him I would have much preferred an error in Bob's denomination to one in his canine preferences, and on and on. It was all in fun, of course, especially considering that Mark towers over me by about a foot and is at least 100 years younger. It took him awhile to comprehend what I was talking about, for when he had written ''Lab'' he was thinking ''retriever.'' The two words were synonyms, even in *his* mind.

From the 1930s to the present, according to AKC registration statistics, the Lab has boasted more popularity every year than all other retriever breeds combined. The Lab has merited this long-term popularity, too, for Lincoln's famous statement about fooling people certainly applies to the sporting breeds.

Originating in Newfoundland (not Labrador) in the nineteenth century, the breed was highly developed in England before being imported to this country early in the twentieth century. Many of the first importers were wealthy sportsmen (Averill Harriman, Marshall Field, Jay Carlisle, et al) who had seen the breed perform in England. These affluent Americans not only brought in the dogs, they also imported professional trainers from the British Isles. The Scot, Dave Elliot, who ''invented'' the blind retrieve, was the premier trainer in the early days. Obviously, the breed was well started in this country, even if its reception in the Chesapeake Bay area was similar to that of Japanese cars in Detroit in more recent times. James Michener covered this quite well in his delightful novel, *Chesapeake,* which should be required reading for every waterfowler.

Labradors have dominated American retriever field trials from the first. Generally, in every stake at every trial, at least 80 percent of the entries are Labs. They have won all but four of the annual National Open Championship trials since their inception in 1941, and every one since 1951. In the annual National Amateur Championship trials, which began in 1957, Labs have won all the titles except for the one in 1985, which was won by a Golden. For all the criticism that field trials have received, they still produce outstanding working retrievers—dogs any waterfowler would be delighted to hunt with. However, they may be guilty of substantial ''overkill,'' in that most field trial training prepares retrievers to handle situations the ordinary hunter would not encounter once in two or three lifetimes. Those critical of these extremes forget that dogs so trained make better day-to-day retrievers than most hunters have ever shot over.

The Labrador's dominance is carrying over into the new hunting retriever tests. Whichever of the three versions you attend, you will see Labs in greater numbers than any other breed, or all other breeds combined.

Ditto for the wildfowl blind. Most hunters who use retrievers use Labs. If you are considering buying your first retriever, and you have no other breed preference, you will likely start out with a Lab, and you will probably

(Adapted from ''A Look at the Lab,'' *Wildfowl,* February/March, 1986.)

be delighted with your choice. They seem to get the job done for anyone who gives them a chance.

So, what is a Labrador like? If I had to describe the breed in one word, that word would be "professional."

The Lab has the dedication, the intensity, and the level of concentration of a professional. When at work, the typical Labrador is in another world. Nothing exists except the birds, the gun, and the dog. At other times the lab can be a pal, a clown, even a lazy bum, but he is all business when hunting.

I remember years ago watching NFC/AFC Butte's Blue Moon running field trials for owner Bing Grunwald and trainer D.L. Walters. Never have I seen such total professionalism in a dog. He pinned the marks and lined the blinds with unbelievable consistency, and was completely oblivious to everything but his job. You could have marched an army or run a pack of hounds through the trial grounds and "Moon" wouldn't have noticed. Yet, I also remember the same dog after his retirement, greeting guests in the Grunwald's home. He didn't look like much of a duck dog there—just a big, old, black house-pet. The criticism that field trials have made soulless robots of the Labrador is ill-founded, and mostly made by people who have only seen the breed at work.

Labradors are the athletes of the retriever world, the ones with the big water entries, the style and dash that catches everyone's eye. Oh, I realize that not every Lab sparkles and shines. Some are slow and plodding—"pigs" is the term for such dogs, whatever the breed—but here we are talking about good Labs, the kind you should be looking for when you buy a pup. Every breed has good ones and bad ones; here I will limit the discussion to the good ones.

The intensity of the Labrador makes training easy for the professional. Other breeds are more personal in their approach to hunting and training; it is very important that they be working for the ones they accept as their masters. The typical Lab couldn't care a spent shell's worth whether it is the boss or a total stranger shooting the birds, as long as they are falling regularly. A good one will work for anyone who can shoot birds and toot the whistle.

However, this intensity *does* create some training problems. It is sometimes difficult to get a Labrador's attention, which makes it necessary for a trainer to get a bit heavy-handed. On the other hand, Labs can absorb more roughness from the trainer than can the other breeds. Again, concentration on their work protects their sensibilities. Retriever training pros have developed training

Labs are so popular that "Lab" is practically a synonym for "retriever."

15

techniques for the breed which may seem harsh to the novice—and which work far less successfully with other breeds—but the Lab generally takes it all in stride. No resentment. No intimidation.

Training the other retriever breeds takes a lot of psychologizing: leading them through it, constantly praising, not putting them down too often, and so forth. I have done this for many years with many dogs, and I must admit that I enjoy it. However, such thoughtfulness has passed over the heads of the Labs I have trained. They have such dedication to their jobs that one need only leave them alone when they are doing things right and correct them enough to get their attention when they goof. Oh, an occasional pat on the shoulder and a "Good dog" helps, of course, but that's about all that is required. Around home it is different. They want as much affection and attention as any other dog. However, when there is work to do, they have little time for the social amenities.

The Labrador also develops earlier than the other retriever breeds. Here there are analogies with other kinds of hunting dogs. The pointer develops faster than the setter, the German Shorthair faster than the Brittany. There are exceptions, I realize, but they are just exactly that—exceptions. For some reason, the short-haired breeds seem to mature faster than the long-hairs.

However, it is also true that the long-hairs tend to stay trained better than the short-hairs. Once a setter is broke, he stays broke. A pointer requires quite a bit of brushing up each year. In dogs, like everything else in life, blessings do not arrive unmixed. The breeds that mature early and train easily require frequent retraining. The breeds that stay trained require more initial time and effort.

Thus it is easy to see why the Lab is the favorite breed among professional trainers. They mature young, train easily, and have to be "redone" frequently. Over the years a pro can make more money training Labradors than he can with other breeds. This is another reason why my one-word description of the breed is "professional"—they are preferred by the pros.

There are three color variations: black, yellow, and chocolate. Blacks are the most popular with field trialers and hunters, but you will see more yellows and chocolates in dog shows. However, there are good hunting Labs available in all colors, so don't let the predominance of blacks dissuade you if you really prefer yellow or chocolate. You can find what you are looking for in any of the three colors.

In hunting, it really doesn't matter which you use. As James Lamb Free indicated in his classic, *Training Your Retriever*, ducks don't flare because of a dog's color. Of course, a dog can attract the birds' attention to the area of the blind, where they may see something else that will spook them, so it is a good idea to keep *any* dog concealed.

Labs have courage, intensity. MHR Lacy Lee Of Lolenda finished her title by running two series on three legs due to torn ligaments. (Photo by Lenda Lee Barker.)

The short coat of the Labrador is deceptive. It hides a dense, woolly undercoat that protects the dog during cold weather. In the spring, when retrievers of all breeds shed, I comb as much hair from my Lab as I do my Golden. Both dogs appear a little fat during winter, but I know that it isn't extra flesh; it's just the protective retriever undercoats.

The short Labrador outercoat has probably gotten a lot of other dogs in trouble, for to the human eye there is little difference between it and the coat of, say, the German Shorthaired Pointer. I remember one occasion when, after giving a retriever demonstration for the Kansas Fish and Game Commission, a young man approached me half outraged because I had made the statement that the retriever breeds' coats protected them from cold water better than those of other hunting breeds. He told me emphatically that his German Shorthair could withstand any water a Lab could and maybe a lot more; that there was no difference in the coats, and on and on.

Now, I have had German Shorthairs—and I love them for Kansas quail—but their coats are not even remotely similar to those of Labs. I tried to explain this, but the young man's mind was made up. I finally cut the discussion short by telling him that just because he didn't mind watching his dog suffer in icy water didn't mean that his dog was not suffering. He didn't like that, but it did shut him up. Unfortunately, it probably didn't teach him

anything, and his unquestionably courageous shorthair probably continues to endure excessively cold water every winter.

That short outercoat of the Lab is nice in the uplands, too, for it seldom requires de-burring. I have spent up to half my hunting time pulling burrs from my Goldens.

The popularity of the Labrador, combined with the outrageous competitiveness of both field trials and dog shows, has split the breed into two sub-breeds: one for field trials and the other for dog shows. Breeders simply don't have the time and money to compete in both areas, nor have they been able to breed sufficient numbers of dogs that could both win in the faddish conditions at dog shows and take the measure of all other entrants in the escalating complexity of field trial tests. While many breeders beat their breasts in remorse over their personal involvements in this reality, and while the more outspoken have never tired of placing all blame in the other camp (bench or field), the real problem lies in the competitive formats of both activities. The new, non-competitive hunting tests represent a giant step toward reversing the process by which this breed split has taken place. Now, all we need is a non-competitive dog show format to match.

Actually, serious breeders have done a remarkable job of maintaining quality in both bench and field Labradors, even though they have not managed to keep it in one breed.

Labs are athletes with big water entries.

17

4

THE LABRADOR RETRIEVER
AND THE RIVER CITY BOYS BAND

Oh, yes, we got trouble with a capital T and that rhymes with P and that stands for Pool.

Change the "P" to "B" and the "Pool" to "Bench" in this line that Professor Harold Hill used to sell the folks of River City a boys band in *The Music Man* and you have the approximate logic that has too often been used to sell copy about hunting dogs, especially when deadlines loom and the mind is in neutral. Any journalist knows the easiest way out of such a situation is to attack. Attack anything. Use half-truths, superstitions, innuendos, whatever, but attack for the full wordcount. No one will notice that the piece is froth and foam. It will sell copy, just as it sold a boys band in River City. The Labrador is an easy target—as is the Golden, another popular breed with a field/bench split. We'll look at a typical diatribe about Labs, but it could be easily reworded to fit several other popular breeds.

You've read the pitch: "We got trouble right here in Labrador Retrievers; that game with the 15 dog show points is the devil's tool; oh, yes, we got trouble; remember The Maine, Shed of Arden, and the golden rule; we surely got trouble. . ."

Such material has frequently placed the Labrador Retriever in a bad light. Thus, when the *Gun Dog* vice-president, Bob Wilbanks, asked me for an assessment of how much trouble the breed is in, I decided this was no time to wing it, or shoot from the hip. I needed the opinions of long-time Labrador experts, people who knew the breed back when and know the breed now; people with enough knowledge to preclude any uninformed prejudice against conformation, field trials, hunting retriever tests, obedience trials, or tracking; well-rounded people whose opinions should be respected. I also needed experts from

different parts of the country. I selected Helen Ginnel, Marianne Foote, and D.L. Walters.

Helen Ginnel of Bedford Hills, New York, has been breeding Labradors in her Whygin kennels since the late 1940s. She is a long-time member of the board of directors of the Labrador Retriever Club, Inc. (LRC), has bred one National Open Field Champion, several field and amateur field champions, many bench champions, as well as many obedience and tracking title holders. She also breeds about 200 pups a year for Guiding Eyes for the Blind.

Marianne Foote of Livermore, California has been breeding Labradors in her Winroc kennels since the late 1950s. Also a long-time member of the LRC board, she has bred one National Amateur Field Champion, several field and amateur field champions, many bench champions, and obedience and tracking title holders. She currently runs some of her dogs in hunting retriever tests.

Professional retriever trainer D.L. Walters of La Cygne, Kansas has been training and field trialing all retriever breeds since the late 1930s and has been a full-time professional since 1945. He has trained and handled two National Open Field Champions, and innumerable field champions. He has also trained many hunting Labradors over the years. He currently employs one full-time assistant for training and trialing field trial dogs, and another full-time assistant training dogs for hunting tests and ordinary hunting.

Now, I know all of you are the right sort of parents; I'm going to be perfectly frank with you: Either you are unaware of the calibre of disaster represented by the presence of a pool table in your midst or . . .

Here, change "pool table" to "bench fancy."

First off, I asked these three Labrador authorities whether there are really two Labrador breeds, one for field and the other for bench. There was no disagreement here: Yes, the breed is split, and has been for a long, long time.

(Adapted from "The Labrador Retriever and the River City Boys Band," *Gun Dog,* November/December, 1987.)

Mrs. Ginnel explained that the real split occurred in post-World War II England, when bench Labrador breeders began developing a stockier, less athletic dog—shorter of leg and neck, more closely coupled through the torso, with a thick tail, and significantly heavier in bone and flesh. Prior to that, both show and field types were basically the same athletic animal we still see in English and American field trials.

For reasons no one really understands, American bench breeders became immediately enamored with these cobbier English show dogs, and began to import them into this country in quantity. Not only did they import the dogs, but they also imported English judges (and still do) to judge Labrador specialties. Now, with English judges appraising mixed classes of English and American dogs, which type do you think won all the marbles? You bet. Thus, American bench breeders were forced to breed the English type to survive in their hobby.

"On the East and West coasts today," Mrs. Ginnel said, "ninety- to ninety-five-percent of the dogs entered in shows are first or second generation English imports."

Mrs. Foote looks at it from a different viewpoint. She said that what you do with a dog will ultimately determine what it looks like. In other words: form follows function. Those who breed field dogs will select sires and dams that are successful in trials; those who breed show dogs will select parents that are successful there. A split is inevitable as long as each sport is so competitive that few can afford the time and money required to win in both.

D.L. Walters talked of a different kind of split, namely one between American and English field Labradors. He explained that our dogs have been bred for many generations as non-slip retrievers, dogs that mark well and take readily to "handling" (blind retrieve training), while the English field dogs are more like spaniels. The English dogs have a lot of that nose-to-the-ground hunting instinct that makes them pleasant upland game dogs. "But," he added, "they're sure hell to get to handle. They don't line or cast far without wandering off to hunt on their own. A good one can be brought around, but it's really a job. Nice dogs for upland game, though."

Mrs. Foote added that retriever trainers and hunters in England and on the European continent are more interested in control and less interested in style than we are. Thus, since (as she previously indicated) form follows function, our dogs are faster and more enjoyable to watch, while the dogs on the other side of the ocean are slower and easier to control.

That game with the 15 numbered balls is the devil's tool.

Here change "numbered balls" to "dog show points."

I asked about the working ability of the bench type Labrador in this country today. D.L. excused himself, explaining that almost all of his experience has been with the field types. (It is refreshing to interview someone who is comfortable saying, "I don't know," when the question is out of his area of expertise.)

Mrs. Ginnel said that a very high percentage of them are capable of anything the average hunter might require. "They are not the athletes the field dogs are, and when sent into the swamp for a duck, a bench dog may take a long time getting there and back, but he can do the work."

Mrs. Foote pointed out that bench breeders in her area (West Coast) have really taken to the new hunting retriever tests, which indicates both that the dogs are capable and that bench breeders are not a collection of irresponsible idiots out to destroy the breed.

I have judged hunting retriever tests on the West Coast and can corroborate what she said. I remember one North American Hunting Retriever Assn. (NAHRA) test I judged in Washington, for example. There were some "typey" Labs in the intermediate and the senior stakes.

Marianne Foote showing Winroc Western Edition to "winners bitch" under judge Carl Tuttle. (Photo by Joan Ludwig, courtesy M. Foote.)

After WWII a cobbier Labrador became popular at dog shows, first in England, then here. This is Ch. Winroc Goforit of Sundalane WC. (Photo by Marianne Foote.)

Not flashy like the field Labradors—and I must admit not my kind of dog, for I prefer retrievers to be fast and stylish—but they were very capable in their own unobtrusive way. I had another opportunity to watch bench Labradors work in the field at a seminar and workshop I conducted for the Greater Denver Labrador Retriever Club in 1986, and I was favorably impressed there, too.

Which brings up a point that no one seems to realize: bench breeders are far more concerned about the working ability of their stock than field breeders are about the conformation of theirs! For example, a member of LRC is not allowed to advertise the show titles of a dog unless the animal has passed a Working Certificate (WC) Test. Granted, the LRC WC Test is very basic—nothing like those of the other retriever breeds, especially the American Chesapeake Club's Working Dog Qualifed (WDQ) Test, which includes a triple mark, a land blind, and a water blind. But, whatever the WC is, it is something positive, and there is no similar stipulation that Labradors with field titles must pass a conformation evaluation.

I have long favored some sort of non-competitive conformation title for field dogs, so I asked my three experts how they felt about it.

Mrs. Ginnel doesn't feel it would be beneficial because it would be too subjective, unlike any kind of field test, in which the dog must do certain things in order to pass.

Mrs. Foote is strongly in favor, pointing out that this sort of thing is done in Germany, where some breed clubs require the following for both sire and dam before a litter can be registered: preformance certificate, conformation certificate, temperament testing certificate, and health certificate. All must be acquired non-competitively.

D.L. feels it would be a good idea, one that would aid in breeding better all-around dogs.

To summarize my findings on the split in the breed: There are two splits, one between bench and field types, the other between American and English field types. However, instead of "ruining" the breed, these splits simply offer three options for the Labrador puppy buyer, and no matter which he chooses, there is a high probability that the dog will be a successful hunter.

An inference from this, which should be painfully obvious to anyone whose IQ is numerically higher than the gauge of his favorite fowling piece, is that no breed has ever been ruined by a bench/field split. As long as there are both types, anyone can find the kind of pup he wants. Only if the field breeders stop breeding will field puppies no longer be available—and no one can blame bench breeders for that. In other words, if there are no (or few) working American Cocker Spaniels today, it is not because bench breeders ruined the breed; it is because field breeders hung it up.

Several breeds are strong and healthy in spite of a complete split between bench and field types. The English Springer Spaniel is really two breeds, but both are doing nicely. Both the Pointer and the English Setter are so completely split between bench and field that the two fancies use different registries (bench-AKC; field-FDSB). Everyone is happy with the arrangement.

Actually, the Labrador is the finest example of a breed that is healthily split and accomplishing wonders in each area. While I personally like to see dual purpose breeds, like several other retriever breeds, I cannot see where two types really hurt anyone or anything, as long as there are good breeders in both camps. If there aren't, then the breed goes the way of the American Cocker, in which the field strain is practically extinct while the bench strain is flourishing. However, who could be so stupid as to blame the bench fancy for the lack of field dogs? Without the bench breeders there wouldn't be any American Cockers at all!

. . . *your son, your daughter, in the arms of animal instinct: MASTERIA!*

Another concern is that of careless breedings by people who know little of genetics, hereditary health problems, conformation, field ability, or anything else. They just, as D.L. puts it, "breed old Shep to old Nell."

Mrs. Ginnel said that this has always been a problem, that there is a lot more of it now because the breed is so

Most bench-bred Labradors can do anything the average hunter might require. (Photo by Marianne Foote.)

popular, but that there are also many more good breedings for the same reason. In other words, there is a lot of garbage out there for those who want ''bargains,'' but there are a lot of gems for those who are more discriminating. You pays yer money and takes yer cherce.

Mrs. Foote also feels that this is a problem, but one the Labrador fancy has a unique control over through the local and regional Labrador clubs (like the Greater Denver LRC, mentioned above) that are flourishing everywhere. These clubs are active and have many knowledgeable members. Fortunately, most of the indiscriminate breeders will eventually try to join such a club, which can only help them out of their ignorance.

D.L. says there are so many good breedings from proven field trial stock available all over the country today that there just is no reason for a person to go to a ''Shep/Nell cross'' for a pup.

In other words: THE PROSPECTIVE LABRADOR OWNER NEVER HAD IT SO GOOD.

Are certain words creeping into his vocabulary, words like . . . 'Swell' and 'So's your old man!'?

Finally, I asked my three experts just how the breed has changed during their years of direct experience, and I received surprising—and surprisingly consistent—answers.

Mrs. Ginnel laughed and said that, other than the change in bench type after World War II, the breed hadn't changed at all—and neither have the gloom-and-doomers. ''In the 50s they were saying things weren't like they were in the 30s; now they are saying the same thing about the 50s. The breed is basically the same as it always has been.''

In other words, things aren't like they were in the good old days, and they never were!

Mrs. Foote said the same thing: The breed hasn't changed, except that there is more of everything now. More good ones, more bad ones, more indifferent ones. She did point out that there is an increased awareness of hereditary health problems today—hips, eyes, blood, shoulders, and so on—and that knowledgeable breeders are working hard to eliminate these problems from their breeding stock, so the long-term outlook is for an even better Labrador.

D.L. said that training techniques have changed but the dogs have remained constant. ''The ones that won in the 40s and 50s—given today's training techniques—would win today.''

''What training techniques?''

''Well,'' he said, ''we do everything so much sooner now: handling, water forcing, and so forth. By the time we have a dog ready for the derby, he's 80 percent ready for the open stake. But come to think of it,'' he chuckled, ''maybe nothing has changed. I remember back in the late 30s watching Freehaven's Jay win the derby and the open at the same trial.''

Thus, I came away with the impression that the breed is unchanged by all of its popularity.

I can deal with the problem with a wave of my hand, this very hand.

What problem, Professor? The breed has tremendous strength in every area, and now can look forward to even more growth in the new hunting tests of one sort and another. I asked my panel what impact these tests would have on the breed.

Mrs. Ginnel and Mrs. Foote both feel that these tests, especially those sponsored by AKC, will be beneficial because they will allow many, many people who lack the time and/or money for competitive field trialing to demonstrate what their dogs can do and have it recorded by the major retriever registry. They also feel that these tests offer the bench fancy something more significant than working certificate tests but more achievable than the field championship and amateur field championship titles.

D.L., who has incorporated hunting retriever test training into his program and taken on a full-time assistant just for that, quite obviously supports the movement. However, he is concerned about the negative propaganda that some of the hunting test leaders have directed toward field trials and field trial breeding.

''They will make a big mistake if they don't build on the good blood that field trialers have developed over the years.''

My overall impression, after talking at length with Mrs. Ginnel, Mrs. Foote, and D.L. Walters, is that the Labrador is showing incredible resilience through this period of expanding popularity; that there are more good ones (however you define good) out there than ever; and that all the parts are in place (local clubs, field trials, hunting tests, working certificate tests, and—yes— conformation shows) to maintain the current quality level indefinitely into the future.

Professor Harold Hill's on hand. River City's gonna have its boys band.

Professor, the pool table doesn't interfere with anyone's billiard game. In fact, it is just another form of recreation under the same roof. If you want to play with your Labrador *your* way, how can you deny the same right to everyone else? River City doesn't need a boys band, and the Labrador doesn't need any more *National Enquirer* journalism.

5

THE GOLDEN RETRIEVER: HANDSOME IS AND HANDSOME DOES

For several years now the Golden has been among the top ten breeds in popularity, according to AKC registration statistics, ranking closely behind the Labrador and considerably ahead of the next most popular retriever, the Chesapeake. The total number of Goldens now living in this country must run several hundred thousand. This popularity has developed since the early 1970s. Prior to that, only the most knowledgeable could even identify the breed—I remember many times being asked about my "funny looking Irish Setters."

Why this relatively sudden popularity? Obviously, the breed's striking good looks played a part. Developed in Scotland in the nineteenth century from a cross between a blond "sport" in a litter of Flat-coated Retrievers and the now extinct Tweed Water Spaniel, the Golden stands about 22- to 25-inches and weighs some 55- to 70-pounds. The retriever with the happy-to-be-alive attitude and the soft, luxurious, gleaming coat—which comes in any golden hue or shade from cream to deep orange—gains immediate attention. But looks are only part of the story. The breed has earned its admirers with deeds, too.

Chronologically, the Golden's rise in popularity in this country happened like this: It was a relatively rare breed until the early 1970s when President Ford brought a Golden female, "Liberty," into the White House. Thereafter, pictures of Liberty appeared everywhere, giving the breed an enormous amount of publicity. Madison Avenue types saw the sales potential underlying this happenstance. They experimented with ads featuring Goldens, and found that these ads worked. Goldens have been hawking everything from soap to automobiles ever since. Even today, one seldom sits through an hour of television, or glances through ten magazine pages without seeing a Golden frolicking on behalf of some product. Thus, almost everyone in the country came to recognize the breed—and many fell in love, and had to have one of their own.

When new owners acquired Goldens, the breed "delivered." They are good all-around hunting dogs as well as marvelous pets. They dominate formal obedience trial competition, both AKC and UKC. They are prominent in AKC dog shows. They excel as guide dogs for the blind. They are even earning the respect of the Labrador field trial set. For example, a Golden, NAFC/FC/AFC Topbrass Cotton (bred, co-owned, and handled by Jackie Mertens) won the 1985 National Amateur Championship trial—the first time any breed other than the Labrador had won it!

People saw. People liked. People bought. AND, the Golden delivered. *That* is how the breed achieved its popularity. While this popularity has split the breed into two types—field and bench—the bench-bred Goldens have retained their working ability. In fact, the working certificate tests sponsored by the Golden Retriever Club of America is much more demanding than that of the Labrador Retriever Club, Inc., and that has helped serious dog show breeders to "keep the 'retrieve' in our retrievers," as they say. Now, the hunting retriever test movement offers additional opportunities to those who want dual purpose dogs.

The Golden is a great hunter, both in the marshes and in the uplands. He is easily trained, easily handled, and he has an unbelievably good nose. In the duck blind the Golden can do it all: handle all the waterfowl you can shoot, and even break skim ice when necessary. Besides, they are good company (quiet, obedient, affectionate) during the long periods of inactivity that characterize duck hunting.

Some feel that the Golden's luxurious coat is a problem in the water, but I have not found that to be the case. A short romp and a few shakes after each retrieve will dry the dog sufficiently for his comfort. As a matter of

(Adapted from "The Golden Retriever," *Gun Dog*, July/August, 1984; "The Golden Retriever," *Dog Fancy*, May, 1986; and "The Golden Retriever," *Wildfowl*, August/September, 1986.)

fact, that lush coat, especially the dense undercoat, provides insulation. Old Duffy, who had a beautiful show coat, often sat by me with icicles hanging all over him without apparent discomfort. He rattled when he moved, but I never saw him shiver. Brandy, another of our Goldens, lacked Duffy's dense undercoat. He shivered in cold weather, but hit the water big every time I sent him for a duck.

Goldens work well on doves, but like all dogs they can become overheated at that time of year. On one occasion, I would have lost Duffy to hyperthermia had there not been a river nearby. When he wobbled in front of me from too much heat, I was able to rush him to the water and lay him down in the shallows. After half an hour of soaking, he was ready to go again, but I had had all the scare I could handle for one day. We went home. Since then I have limited my dove hunting to ponds; no more waking the birds up along hedgerows.

Goldens make excellent flush dogs in the uplands, as do most retrievers. True, they are not as light-footed and merry as the English Springer Spaniel on pheasants, grouse, and such birds. Nor are they as breathtaking on quail as a pointing dog. Nevertheless, if a guy wants to hunt everything with one dog—waterfowl and upland game birds—a Golden can handle the job as effectively as any dog, and better than most.

The Golden coat can be a problem in the uplands, for it seems to attract stickers and burrs like a magnet. While the owner can normally wait until the end of the day to pull them out, I remember once when I had to stop and de-burr Duffy about every half-hour, and it took me about fifteen minutes each time. My son Bob's golden, Brandy, pulled his own burrs, so it was only necessary to pluck those he couldn't reach: under his chin and on his neck. I've asked Bob how he trained Brandy to do that, but he won't tell me!

My one-word description of the Golden is "personable." The typical Golden has a bright, happy outlook, perhaps reflecting a very good self-image. He seems convinced that he is quite a nice fellow and that any person or other dog around will surely realize it.

Over the years we have had two Golden female housepets. Through most of the years of their residency, our five kids were growing up, so we had a constant stream of young humanity passing through the place. First Cindy and later Tina enjoyed this immensely, and it was impossible for any one to spend even a few minutes in our house without petting the dog. Even those who professed to dislike animals found themselves unconsciously scratching an ear or chin, without noticing the nudging and nuzzling that initiated it.

Fortunately, we never had a burglary, for I'm sure that either Cindy or Tina would have greeted the thief as warmly as they did any other visitor. As a matter of fact, if a burglar could communicate what he is looking for to the average Golden, the dog would probably help him find it. Goldens are a washout as watchdogs.

They get along well with other dogs, being more interested in making friends and playing than in bluffing and blustering. If another dog bristles, the Golden will offer the olive branch. I have seen Goldens take an awful amount of physical abuse from small, feisty dogs without retaliation. However, even a Golden has his limits. If another dog large enough to constitute a real threat attacks him, it's Katie-Bar-The-Door. Once a fight is forced on him, the Golden exercises no more restraint. It is a total commitment.

Pro trainer D.L. Walters told me that he has never seen a Golden start a fight, but that when attacked, he is really vicious: breaking bones, tearing hide, mutilating. D.L. said a couple of Labs might roll around on the ground, growl, and look tough, but they usually won't hurt each other. Goldens, on the other hand, fight to the finish, inflicting serious injuries. I have no personal experience with Goldens in fights—thank heaven—but then I keep my Goldens away from hostile dogs.

Goldens love to be trained, as long as the approach is positive. They want so much to please that they respond to positive techniques very nicely—heavy-handed measures simply have no place. Some people are not temperamentally suited to this kind of dog. Those who are hard-boiled, aloof, or perhaps a little vindictive should seek another breed.

Goldens mature much more slowly than Labradors, but a tad to a bunch more rapidly than the other retriever breeds. While Labradors are the pro's dogs, Goldens are better trained by their owners. True, Goldens can be professionally trained, and many have been through the years, but both pro and owner must understand that it takes longer and therefore costs more.

The control side of training—obedience and blind retrieves—is where the Golden really comes into his own. A Golden loves to learn new ways to please the boss, and the more the boss shows his pleasure, the faster the dog learns. Moreover, the Golden, once he is fully trained, obeys happily. He is far less likely than the Lab to "get a better idea" and turn his handler off. The Golden may get an idea of his own, of course, but pleasing the boss means so much to him that he will respond to the boss's directions even when they go against the dog's own instincts.

There is a saying among field trialers that a Golden loves to be "handled" (to a blind retrieve), a Chesapeake resents it, and a Lab doesn't much care one way or the other. A good Golden is hard to beat on a blind retrieve, and if he happens to be marking well on a given day, he is tough to beat, period. The opposite is true of the Chesapeake. He is tough to beat in marking, and on the day he happens to accept handling, he will pick up all the marbles. The Lab doesn't excel at either, but his overall

Goldens "deliver."

performance is good enough to win most trials. Success in field trials is much like success in golf: more dependent on mistakes than on excellence. And Labs make fewer mistakes.

In any kind of training, a Golden requires a strongly positive, supportive approach from the trainer. He needs lots of reassurance that he is doing it right, pleasing the boss. Given that, he will do outstanding work. Denied it, he will take measures, and the measures will vary depending on whether his owner or a pro is doing the training.

With his owner, the under-appreciated Golden will sulk and refuse to cooperate. He feels he should be part of a closely-knit team that is almost a mutual admiration society. If denied that status, he will stop playing the game.

Years ago a young Golden named Mickey (mentioned earlier as something less than the brightest dog I have ever trained) gave me a lesson in this tactic. One evening he had problems with his "Over" cast to the left, even though he had done it well the previous day. After a couple of failures, I blew my stack. I really unloaded on the dog—to the point that I am right now embarrassed to think of it. Mickey stopped doing *anything* for me, no matter how rough I got with him. He stonewalled it. Had I gone back a few steps and led him through it, we would have had a good session. As it was, I made the evening a complete failure. (I handled things more appropriately the next night, and a forgiving Mickey performed well.)

With a professional trainer, a Golden whose dignity has been offended beyond tolerance can be a menacing problem. One pro almost lost a thumb this way. The Golden seemed to turn him off on a blind retrieve, ignoring the whistle, running wild. Not realizing that the dog had run afoul of some fire-ants, the outraged pro took off after the animal. When he caught him, he reached for the dog's neck with one hand and started winding up his whip with the other. In pain from fire-ant bites, the Golden had no intention of taking a whipping, too. He lunged up at the hand that was reaching for him and ripped the thumb almost completely off. Fortunately, a surgeon was able to restore it at the hospital.

Another pro, who had been training retrievers (90 to 95 percent Labradors) for forty years at the time, told me that he had about thirty dog-bite scars on his arms, and that most of them came from Goldens.

The point is that while a Golden may be a "soft" dog, there is a boundary beyond which he will not be pushed. He has his dignity, and the trainer had better respect it. Frankly, the typical Golden responds so well to positive training techniques that rough stuff is usually out of place.

Just as there is no such thing as an all-around hunting dog, so there is no such thing as one breed for everyone, even within the limits of a particular type of hunting (like

Two Golden pups learning about birds. A little of this kind of play goes a long way.

Goldens are wonderful in the house. Here is Rumrunner's Abbie, bred by the author, at 13 years. (Photo by Linda Page.)

waterfowling). Whether the Golden is the dog for you depends on the kind of person you are. If you are affectionate and outgoing, you will get along well with the breed. If you are more reserved and undemonstrative, you might be better off with a Lab.

If you really object to digging burrs from a dog's coat, by all means do not buy a Golden. On the other hand, if you feel that having a dog that is easy to train, easy to handle, that excels in running down crippled birds is worth the effort necessary to untangle a few burrs every hunting day, a Golden might be the dog for you.

If you need a watchdog, forget the Golden. For all their dignity with professional trainers, they are too friendly around home for those needing canine protection. However, if you have a "busy" house, with lots of human traffic, a Golden will be a good PR representative for your entire family.

If you are interested in field trials, you should probably buy a Lab. If you intend to enter the new hunting retriever tests, you could make do nicely with a Golden. They are running a distant second to Labs in success there, but the movement is new, and I feel that the Golden will match the Lab in these non-competitive tests within a few years—perhaps eventually dominating them like they do obedience trials.

If you just plain like Goldens but feel you may not be the ideal owner, go ahead and get one. He'll bring you around in no time. Goldens are as good as people trainers as they are as trainees.

Goldens are great hunters. FC/AFC Barty's Sunshine Express brings in a duck. Owned by Linda Daley. (Photo by D. Milne, courtesy "The Prince George Citizen.")

6

THE CHESAPEAKE BAY RETRIEVER: AMERICAN MAGNUM WILDFOWLER

Chesapeakes aren't for everyone."
Ask any Chessy owner whether you should get a Bay dog and that is probably the first statement he/she will make. The owners of almost any other sporting breed will give you an unqualified endorsement. You know the routine: great pet, outstanding hunter, perfect watchdog, smartest canine there ever was, beautiful, faithful, will fetch your slippers, set out your decoys, and even shoot your birds if you are having an off day.

But Chessy owners will be more cautious, more circumspect. They'll tell you that their dogs can be difficult, that they are independent, and sometimes a bit cantankerous. Not for everyone; that's for sure.

And there are always stories to go with the caution. The pro who had to use a garbage can lid as a shield when punishing a Chesapeake. The Chessy that ''treed'' two pros on top of their truck when they tried to use an electronic collar on him. And on and on.

Not for everyone. Yet the very people who say this most often are fanatically devoted to the breed. If you doubt that, just make an unkind remark about the Bay dog in their company. Then you will find out what they really think of the breed: best foul-weather dog on earth; tough, fearless, tireless; unbelievable markers; the only breed to have in the blind with you when the chips are down and the odds are against you; something special.

Special, unique, difficult to explain. That is the Chesapeake Bay Retriever. Developed in this country, the Chessy is all Yankee. There is not an English or European trait in his make-up, and perhaps that is why he is so difficult to define, for our canine frame of reference is English and European. To understand the Chessy, you must understand the American character as it has developed over the past four or five centuries, and partic-

ularly as it evolved during the nineteenth and early twentieth centuries, when the Bay dogs were developed. If there is any truth to the saying that a nation develops dogs that closely resemble its people, I can better understand the mixed reviews we Americans get overseas, even when we are trying to be friendly.

The Chesapeake stands tall and carries plenty of muscle; he is larger and more powerful than the other retrievers. While sizes vary from about 22- to 28-inches and 55 to well over 100 pounds, most Chessies are large, and all of them are strong for their size. When I steadied my then 80-pound (now 95-pound) Bay dog, Beaver, he hit the end of the belt cord so hard so often that I worried that he would stretch my left arm a few inches. Sometimes it felt like I had lassoed a fast freight. These dogs were developed to retrieve ducks and geese from Chesapeake Bay all day and even into the night back when there were no limits, so their size and strength should be no surprise. Even today a wildfowler looking for a goose dog has a better chance of getting what he wants—a dog that will tangle with and subdue a tough, old, crippled giant Canada—if he opts for the breed from the Bay. That is not to say that the other breeds do not produce good goose dogs, but when a guy shops among litters of untried puppies, he should go with the smart money and bet on the Chessy.

The Chesapeake has a marvelous double coat which is more suited to really bad weather than those of the other retrievers. His slightly waved but harsh and oily outercoat hides a wooly, water-resistant undercoat, and the combination will normally keep his skin dry even after hours of retrieving. Most retriever breeds have double coats, but not like the Chessy's. The pungent aroma of his oily outercoat may occasionally make him less than welcome in the confines of the living room, but it smells like perfume to a duck hunter when the dog brings in a cripple after a long chase.

(Adapted from ''Chesapeake Bay Retrievers,'' *Wildfowl,* June/July, 1986.)

Originally, the dogs were dark brown, but the lighter "dead grass" color was developed somewhere along the way to better camouflage the dog. Dogs, in and of themselves, do not disturb birds, although they may attract the birds' attention to the vicinity of the blind, where something else may spook them. Thus, every retriever, regardless of color should be tucked away out of sight. Color is irrelevant. I like the dark ones. If you like the lighter hues, fine. We can both be happy.

The overall conformation of the breed is functional rather than beautiful. This standard calls for the rump to be as high as or higher than the wither—great for waterwork but not as elegant in the show ring as the sloping back of the setters. For those hunters who feel that "handsome is as handsome does," the Chessy is gorgeous above all other breeds, for one look tells you the dog "can do." He is not as pretty as a Golden or as sleek as a Labrador, but he catches your eye nevertheless. He isn't the fleet-footed scatback or wide receiver. He's more the pulling guard, the linebacker, or the tight end, and he has his own poetry, his own meter.

While not every Chesapeake has dog show conformation, the breed has not been split into two distinct types, as have both the Labrador and the Golden. The Chessy has never achieved the level of popularity that normally precedes such a split. Further, good Chesapeake conformation lacks the striking beauty which appeals to those who limit their involvement to conformation competition. While not every hunting Chessy is show quality, those that appear in the show ring also hunt.

The Chessy is mentally as well as physically tough. He attacks a job with a single-minded determination and a sense of self-confidence that makes him difficult to dissuade. He marks well, remembers well, and has the cunning to deal with most situations that come up in a day's waterfowling, so he prefers to hunt with someone who will allow him some latitude. He seems to say, "You call and shoot the bird, and then leave the rest to me. I won't interfere with your job if you won't interfere with mine." Handling a Chessy with whistle and arm signals, especially if he thinks he knows where the bird fell, is apt to be difficult. Even on a blind retrieve, you had better put him on the bird quickly or he will decide he can find it quicker on his own, and turn you off. He is a free spirit that wants to do his own job his own way, without having the boss breathing down his neck all the time.

The Chesapeake loves water so much that sometimes it seems they would rather swim than walk. I have always introduced Goldens and Labradors to water very carefully. After all, these breeds were developed as land retrievers in England and have only been adapted to American waterfowling in this century. The Chessy was developed as a water dog from the start so takes to this medium almost as well as he does to land. When Beaver was a little puppy, he dove into the first farm pond I showed

The Chesapeake was developed for waterfowling in bad weather.

him, swam about forty yards, and tried to uproot a small dead tree. No cautious introductions were needed for Beaver.

While they excel as water dogs—the best breed for the person who hunts only waterfowl—they are less than spectacular in the uplands. Many refuse to work ahead of the hunter to flush birds, preferring to amble along beside the boss until he finds "respectable" work (retrieving). Others will adequately hunt to the gun, but without the enthusiasm of the other retriever breeds.

The Chesapeake's temperament makes him a good friend and a bad enemy. If he accepts you as one of his people, he will die for you or kill for you. He will protect you, sometimes when you don't really need it, which can be embarrassing.

I remember a Saturday many years ago at pro D.L. Walters' grounds. I had lunch with Marge and Sam Woolsey in their fifth-wheeler, which was always parked there in those days. While Marge was busy in the kitchen area, Sam and I were sitting on the sofa. Their young Chessy jumped up on the sofa between Sam and me. He didn't look left or right, just sat there staring straight ahead. As the three of us talked, I unconsciously reached up to scratch the dog's chin. Still looking straight ahead, he started a low growl that told me I had just made a mistake. I pulled my hand away slowly, but that didn't change a thing. The dog continued to growl, almost inaudibly, I could hear him, believe me, for he had my attention. The growl was so soft that Sam didn't notice it until I told him that his dog was about to have me for lunch.

It took the author 2.5 months to force-break Beaver!

Chessies are tough enough to handle big geese, as Beaver does here.

Sam ordered the dog to lie down on the other side of the room. The dog obeyed, but he never took his eyes off me all the time I was there. Later, I figured out what the problem was: That young Chessy hadn't jumped up on the sofa to be sociable; he was protecting Sam from a stranger (me).

Understanding that protective quality is crucial to getting along with Chessies. If you don't know the dog, don't "violate his space" or that of his owner. Actually, that is a pretty good rule to follow with any dog of any breed. However, the rube who just has to show what a great hand he is with dogs runs a greater risk of ending up with a punctured epidermis if he takes uninvited liberties with a Chesapeake than he does with most other sporting breeds. On the other hand, the person who uses common sense, allows the dog to make the initial overtures, and even then takes it easy until the dog is comfortable, will have little difficulty with most Chessies. A Chesapeake forms definite opinions about people and chooses his friends cautiously. They have a strong sense of dignity, and insist that friend and enemy alike respect that dignity.

My one-word description for the breed is "passionate." They love with great intensity. They hate the same way. Even their indifference toward strangers has

passion in it: their steely eyes communicate, "You had better leave me alone, buddy!"

Because of this passionate nature, a Chessy is best trained by his owner, that one human being the dog totally accepts. The dog will do things simply to please that one person that no amount of punishment could induce him to do for anyone else.

Sure, a good pro can train a Chesapeake, but it will not be easy. The reason the breed has the reputation for being tough, hard-headed, independent, and just plain mean is that they don't really give much of a damn what anyone thinks except for that one special man or woman. A pro can use training techniques that work nicely on a Lab, but the Chessy couldn't care less what the pro wants, so he doesn't respond like Labs do. Sometimes a pro can get rough enough to gain grudging compliance, but more often the dog just endures the pain and continues to figuratively flip off the pro.

Further, the breed matures more slowly than the Golden—much more slowly than the Labrador. Thus, he doesn't fit the pace of a professional program built around these breeds. He needs to be trained at his own rate of speed, and no one can better assess that than his owner, who has (or at least should have) frequent daily interaction with the dog.

The best way to involve a pro in the training of a Chesapeake is for the owner to train the dog under the pro's guidance. (Most pros have a fee structure for this kind of work.) It allows the dog to learn new ways to please the boss; it allows the boss to learn how to train the dog. And it saves the pro the problems he would have in motivating a dog that is passionately indifferent in the normal pro/dog relationship.

Now, I'll let you in on the best kept secret of Chessy training: They are a soft breed! Yeah, those big, rough and tumble heaps of vibrating muscle mass, those tough critters that show no sign of fear when subduing an equally tough giant Canada, those weather-proof ice-breakers that seem not to notice the difference between an early bluebird day and a late-season blizzard, those unbelievably tough Chesapeake Bay Retrievers are soft and sensitive to the approval or disapproval of their owners. In this characteristic they are the equal of the Golden Retriever.

Train a Chessy like you would a Golden, with lots of praise and appreciation, and your training will be easy. Use the harsher approach that works well with the Labrador and he will turn you off—in fact, he may turn on you if you push him too far. Where the Golden will sulk and quit, the Chesapeake will sulk and brood.

Many women have been successful Chesapeake trainers because of their greater sensitivity to the animal's need for praise and appreciation. I have to chuckle when I hear someone say the Chessy is the ideal dog for the hard-boiled, heavy-handed, macho man. Actually, the Chessy is the worst possible dog for such a person, for the dog probably won't accept his training program, and he may take the guy apart under stress.

This doesn't mean that a Chesapeake won't accept correction. He will, but it should be within the framework of positive motivation, and the dog should understand what he did wrong. Then the owner's disapproval may be heavy enough punishment. Of course, when the animal openly defies authority, as every Chesapeake frequently does, the boss must assert himself.

While the Chessy craves constant approval as much as the Golden, his approach is uniquely "Chesapeake-ish." Where the Golden strives to do everything the boss's way, the Chesapeake likes to "fight and make up." He challenges the boss's authority at almost every training session, and seems delighted when the boss asserts himself. In fact, the dog will continue to challenge until the boss does indeed clamp down on him.

I cannot remember a single training session in which I didn't have to " 'splain it to Beaver so's he could understand it" at least once. His favorite trick is to drop a bird at my feet rather than deliver it to hand. Now, he has been force-broken (which took 2½ months!), so he knows better. He also knows that I will make his upper lip hurt every

time he pulls this stunt. Nevertheless, at least once per session, he drops a bird beside me and looks up as if to say, "It's that time again, boss. Don't blame me for my nature. I have to do this, and neither of us knows why. If you wanted a Golden Retriever, you should have bought a Golden Retriever." Then, I force him to pick it up and hold it, after which he seems satisfied, and bears no resentment. I pat him on the shoulder to show there are no hard feelings—which is very important to every Chesapeake—and we go on with training as if the challenge had never happened.

I have a saying: You train a Golden; you distract a Labrador; you negotiate with a Chesapeake.

The most important part of that negotiation comes right after you have won the debated point. If you remain angry, the dog will grow resentful. If you forgive and give him a buddy-buddy pat on the shoulder, he will worship you. You are then the benevolent boss, the kind-hearted tyrant that a Chesapeake needs. I have often uttered "Good boy!" through tightly clenched teeth as my blood pressure pounded in my temples.

A Chesapeake can be a problem around other dogs. While I've seen them romping and playing together like a bunch of lap dogs, I do not allow Beaver freedom around dogs he doesn't know. He's fine with his kennel-mates,

You negotiate with a Chessy.

30

and he has never been in a fight in his life. I want to keep it that way, so I am careful with him.

It may seem that I am saying, ''Chessies are not for everyone,'' just as so many other Chesapeake owners do. Maybe I am, but I am not disparaging the breed. I want to make sure that each Chesapeake pup finds a ''proper'' owner—one who understands ALL the breed's characteristics and finds them not only acceptable but fascinating.

Who is this ideal owner? Well, first he/she should be a dedicated wildfowler, a fanatic rather than a dabbler. A practical bent of mind is an advantage, too. For example, when someone asks you what is the most beautiful shotgun ever manufactured, if you're stuck trying to decide whether it is the boxy old Browning Automatic,

the exposed-hammer Winchester 97 pump, or the newer behemouth, the Ithaca Mag-10, you're probably Chesapeake material. The Chessy type admires a gun that can take it and take it and take it and still nail the next duck or goose stone dead.

He also prefers doing his own training rather than farming the job out to a pro. He will accept the passionate, protective nature of the breed and be willing to see that these traits don't get the animal in trouble. That means having proper kenneling at home and maintaining reasonable control while training and hunting.

I guess what I am saying is that the Chesapeake Bay Retriever may not be for everyone, but he might be just right for you.

Chessies have marvelously protective coats. (Photo courtesy Maryanne Foote.

31

7

THE FLAT-COATED RETRIEVER: "TO THINE OWN SELF BE TRUE"

This breed has always possessed remarkable integrity, primarily because it has been supported by breeders dedicated to its integrity.

Integrity consists of three components: correctness, wholeness, and longevity. Correctness in relation to some uncompromising standard of excellence. Wholeness in the sense that each quality part meshes nicely into a quality whole. And longevity, for short-lived correctness and wholeness may not stay the course.

First, let's look at the Flat-Coat's longevity. They have been picking up downed birds for British wingshooters as long as any of the several retriever breeds, and were the most popular from the earliest days until World War I. Since that time, the breed's popularity has fallen significantly behind first the Labrador and later the Golden. Several reasons have been alleged for the Flat-Coat's reduced numbers through that period: the more rapid maturity of the Labrador; the introduction of competitive field trials; the striking looks of the Golden Retriever; and perhaps a few others.

However, there is another seldom-mentioned reason, one that addresses the correctness and wholeness of the breed, one that is most significant in explaining why the Flat-Coat has never achieved great popularity in post-World War I England or the USA, and perhaps never will: The breeders refused, and still refuse, to split the breed into two types, one for competitive field trials and the other for competitive conformation shows. Competition leads naturally to specialization, as is demonstrated by so many sporting breeds that have been split into two types: field and show.

This is not the case with the Flat-Coat, and I hope that never changes. The Flat-Coats that succeed in field trials, hunting retriever tests, and working certificate tests,

generally win in conformation shows, too. True, most of the conformation wins are strictly within the breed itself, not in the Sporting Group, where uselessly long and nicely barbered coifs seem to generate more enthusiasm than practical hunting coats.

Flat-Coat fanciers have never become so dedicated to winning at any price that they would sacrifice the breed's integrity. Thank God for people like that. Thus, the Flat-Coat today is a true dual dog: good-looking and good-working. The breeders, both in England and in this country, have maintained the Flat-Coat's correctness and wholeness for a long time. Thus, the breed has integrity.

Conditions are changing in ways that may benefit these patient breeders and the breed they have nurtured so carefully. More on this later. First, let's look at the physical and mental make-up of the dog.

The Flat-Coat is an average-sized dog, about 24 inches at the withers, weighing 60- to 70-pounds. While the breed resembles the other retrievers more than it does setters, it does have a "setter-ish" quality, in that it is a bit taller, thinner and "finer" in the head than the other retrievers. It also has a setter-like loftiness in its movement.

The coat, which is usually all black, but which may also be all liver, is longer and softer than that of the Labrador, but much shorter and less abundant than that of the Golden.

Breeder/trainer Bunny Milikin of Andover, Massachusetts, says "The Labrador has twice as many hairs per square inch, and the Golden has four times as many. The Flat-Coat has a nice, shake-dry coat."

Predictably, burrs are more of a problem with a Flat-Coat than with a Labrador, but much less so than with a Golden. "The typical Flat-Coat will pull most of his own burrs out," says breeder/trainer Sally Terroux of Arvada, Colorado. "When you get him out of the crate, there will be a neat little pile of burrs in one corner."

(Adapted from "The Flat-Coated Retriever," *Wildfowl*, June/July, 1987.)

A breed of integrity. Ch. Dynamite's Anxious Arrival CDX. (Photo by Cott/Francis, courtesy Sally Terroux.)

On the other hand, the dark colors make the breed heat-sensitive, even more so than the shorter-coated Labrador. Dove hunters must be careful to avoid overheating the Flat-Coat on warm days. Conversely, this dark coat seems to protect the dog in cold weather and even in cold water much better than one would think, judging from its moderate length and density.

The Flat-Coat has a high energy level all through his typically long life. Even geriatric dogs are playful, still able to hunt. Because he has so much energy, a Flat-Coat is very apt to "take a romp" on the first bird he retrieves after a long period of confinement. The dog locates the bird, but instead of picking it up immediately, he runs vigorously around and around within the area of the fall until he feels physically relieved, and then he makes a normal retrieve. People who travel long distances to hunt or run tests or trials are most apt to encounter this problem. All breeds do it, of course—a Golden of mine (Brandy) once sank to third in a field trial he would have won had he not taken a romp on the first bird—and the only way to prevent it is to avoid long confinements just before working the dog. Really, it is a handler's error, for no dog should be snatched from the crate and sent after a retrieve without some preliminary exercise.

The breed appears to be physically tough, able to withstand pain and discomfort afield quite well. However, this may be more a manifestation of his intense desire to work than of any innate physical insensitivity to pain. Sally Terroux does a lot of "puppy sensitivity testing" with her litters, and she has found that Flat-Coats are actually more sensitive physically than the other retriever breeds she has tested. She attributes the Flat-Coat's apparent toughness to extreme birdiness; they become too absorbed in hunting and retrieving to notice normal pain and discomfort. They will drive through the nastiest cover in the uplands, break ice time after time to retrieve ducks, and generally punish themselves as necessary to get the job done.

They love water. Most puppies require only minimal introduction to it before they will gleefully jump in every time they get near it.

Noses vary, of course, as they do in all breeds, but on the average, the Flat-Coat olfactory capabilities rival those of the Golden, which is about as good as they get among retrievers.

My one-word description of the breed is, "elegant." The Flat-Coat personality is absolutely charming, whether around the house or in the field. They are bright and happy,

33

glad to be with their owners, gracious but not demanding with visitors, and great companions for all the neighborhood kids.

The greatest need of the typical Flat-Coat is a strong bond with his owner. He is a house dog rather than a kennel dog, and must have daily interaction with the boss—''Quality time,'' as Sally Terroux puts it. This interaction may take the form of games (whatever sort the owner chooses will do nicely), or just walking and talking around the place. In short, anything with activity and companionship will do. A Flat-Coat is not satisfied with an occasional pat on the head by the fireplace while the boss reads and sips. There must be physical involvement and activity.

The Flat-Coat is naturally competitive with other dogs, although not inclined to quarrel. Thus, the Flat-Coat is most comfortable when he is the only dog in his owner's life. He can live happily with one or two other dogs, but more than that make it difficult for him to receive the kind of attention he needs.

A typical specimen is very birdy and has an insatiable desire to retrieve. These traits, combined with his affection for his owner, make him a very stylish performer, both going out and returning. In early 1986 I judged a working certificate (WC and WCX) test conducted by the

''Quality time.'' (Photo by Sally Terroux.)

Flat-coats love water. Ch. Kelly's Gamble CDX WC, owned by Robert and Joan Sharpe. (Photo by Sandra Etherington Tucker, courtesy Sally Terroux.)

Golden Retriever Club of America. Two Flat-Coats were entered—since the requirements are identical for both national breed clubs—among the large field of Goldens. One was Tealsnest Ptarmigan, owned by Ron Wickhorst, and the other was Ch. Tealsnest Topsail Trover CDX, owned by Pete Baum. I have been a Golden fancier since I first shot over one back in the late 1940s, and I will remain one all my life. However, the dogs that impressed me in that test—the ones I saw that night when I closed my eyes—were those two merry Flat-Coats. They were more than stylish; they had what bird dog folks call "class." This may well derive from their setter-like carriage. Those two Flat-Coats were fast, snappy, good markers, with big water entries—and they were beautifully put together. Trover broke on the honor in the WCX (perhaps demonstrating the breed's competitiveness), but I would have gladly smuggled him home with me. He has since successfully completed his WCX in another test, which gives him a field title to go with his bench and obedience titles.

The breed possesses good bird sense. In the uplands he learns quickly where the birds hang out. Even in tracking cripples he learns to play the odds as well as use his nose. Such uncanny bird sense makes him a bit strong-minded sometimes, for he prefers to trust his own instincts, judgement, and experience rather than heed the insistent "tweeeet" coming from the boss's whistle.

They mature much more slowly than Labradors, a little more slowly than Goldens. Thus, the trainer must learn to "wait on nature" (as herding breed trainers say). He must make the early work lots of fun, saving the pressure for when the dog matures sufficiently to be able to cope with it. Throughout the dog's life, training must be positive, with ample praise for success, and only mild corrections for failures. The dog must feel appreciated.

The harsh techniques that bring out the best in the Labrador will destroy the Flat-Coat. Sally Terroux advises her puppy buyers to join Golden training groups (since there are so few Flat-Coat groups) and learn the gentler approaches they use. She also tells them that the first prerequisite for Flat-Coat training is bonding, for training is very personal with the breed. As insane as he is to retrieve, he will not do it for just anyone. In fact, without a strong bond, the trainer will experience great difficulty dealing with the dog's combination of sensitivity and independence.

According to Bunny Milikin, Flat-Coats mark and "count" quite well. This means that they excel in estimating the location of a fallen bird, and that they remember several falls long enough to retrieve all of them, one at a time. Most have a lot of "hunt" in their make-ups, which means that if they don't find a bird immediately, they will use their noses and eyes to search the area in which it fell until they do find it.

These traits are not unmixed blessings, for dogs that mark, count, and hunt well normally challenge the trainer's patience in blind retrieve work. The Flat-Coat would rather go off and hunt for the bird he didn't see fall than accept whistle and arm signals. However, an insistent but patient boss will eventually win this controversy, although the Flat-Coat may "forget" occasionally all his life.

The typical Flat-Coat dislikes lengthy, repetitive drills—the kind of training that polishes the Labrador so well. The Flat-Coat bores easily, so needs something new each session. However, as every trainer knows, training is conditioning, and conditioning demands repetition. Good trainers solve this paradox by doing a few repetitions of several different exercises (a mark, a lining drill, and a casting drill, for example) during each session, relying on many sessions to condition the dog. Most dogs, regardless of breed, have a "magic number" of repetitions they will accept at one time before starting to resist. It will seldom be less than four or more than seven. The trainer must assume responsibility for learning what that magic number is for each of his dogs—and for respecting it.

Most Flat-Coats benefit from plenty of fun mixed in with the serious training. The knowing trainer will end each session with a couple of "fun dummies": retrieves in which the dog is encouraged to break and chase as the trainer throws the dummy. Ending each session this way gives the dog something pleasant to remember until the next session.

Until recently there really hasn't been a place for the Flat-Coat in our American scheme of things. The Labrador dominates field trials. The Golden dominates obedience trials. Several flashier breeds dominate dog shows. A few Flat-Coats have done well in all these activities, but most just don't fit the molds. The fancy has refused to breed an imitation Labrador for field trialing, or a floor-wiping coat for dog shows. They have bred their Flat-Coats true, enjoying them privately and quietly. However, perhaps their patience and integrity are about to be rewarded.

The hunting retriever movement offers an excellent non-competitive opportunity to earn respectable titles and demonstrate the breed's impressive abilities to the general hunting public. Flat-Coat owners are beginning to enter these tests. All that is lacking for the full promulgation of the virtues of this breed is a similar non-competitive dog show format in which fads of coat length, topline, and tonsorial art play no part. Conformation titles could be awarded like hunting test titles, based on compliance with the standard. The combination of a non-competitive field title and a non-competitive conformation title would assure breeders and puppy buyers that a dog is a true dual dog: good working, physically sound, and representative of the breed.

The AKC maintains a written standard of perfection for every breed it recognizes. In fact, the name "conformation" derives from the fact that in dog shows the competing dogs are judged by how well they "conform" to that written standard. One can only hope that the AKC will one day realize how much the non-competitive format has done for hunting tests and obedience trials—especially in reducing the cost of participation—and introduce it into dog shows, too. No other sporting breed is in a better position to take advantage of such an opportunity than the Flat-Coat.

What kind of person should own a Flat-Coat? First, he/she should want a house dog rather than a kennel dog, for no one gets much from a Flat-Coat that is isolated away from frequent human contact. Such a dog doesn't bond, and the Flat-Coat that doesn't bond doesn't work.

The potential owner should limit himself to one or two dogs, three at the most. More than that will result in a neglected Flat-Coat, unless the Flat-Coat is the sole house dog while the other animals are kept in outside kennel runs.

The Flat-Coat owner must be an outgoing, expressive person, one from whom expressions of praise and appreci-

ation come easily. He must be one not given to anger, carping, or nagging.

Anyone with a fixed training schedule tatooed in his subconscious should avoid the Flat-Coat. They are slow maturing, and their owners must be willing to wait on nature. Forget the "On the eighty-fourth day your dog is ready for . . ." stuff, and train according to the Flat-Coat's evolving ability to understand and cope. Training should be relaxed fun for both trainer and trainee, not a psychological track meet.

Finally, the potential Flat-Coat owner should accept the high standards that serious breeders have maintained through the years. The breed's integrity is much easier to lose than maintain. Integrity is like virginity, too, in that once lost, it is never regained. The person interested in only one phase of retriever work, field *or* bench, can choose from the breeds that are already split along those lines (Labrador and Golden). Why upset what serious Flat-Coat breeders have worked so hard to uphold?

There is no better way to close this profile of the Flat-Coat than to quote a line from *Hamlet:* "This above all—to thine own self be true, and it must follow as the night the day, that thou canst not then be false to any man."

Flat-coats have good upland hunting bird sense. (Photo by Bunny Milikin.)

8

THE CURLY-COATED RETRIEVER: ENGLISH MAGNUM WILDFOWLER

The current growth of our geese populations may do for the Curly-Coated Retriever what it has already done for the 10-gauge magnum shotgun.

The breed is rare in this country. However, many American waterfowlers, especially geese afficionados, would find the Curly ideal if they knew a little more about him. Granted, the Chesapeake is doing fine work, thank you, for many goose hunters—and few would question the Chessy's superiority at subduing hostile honkers. However, not everyone shares my personal fondness for the Chessy, so there is room for another big, rough-and-tumble retriever. Besides, the typical Curly surpasses the typical Chessy as an upland flusher.

Two things prevent the Curly from realizing the popularity his abilities would seem to deserve: ignorance of the breed's place among retrievers; and unfounded assumptions about its armorlike, burr-resistant coat.

Let's look at this British 10-bore retriever, to see what he could do in this country, and to determine what adjustments we might have to make in our thinking to get the most from him. To do this, we will have to compare him to the retriever breeds with which we are more familiar. While I agree with Emerson that "comparisons are odious," I must concede that they are also damned handy in most learning processes. The comparisons I make here should not be construed as attempts to rank the relative merits of the various breeds. I am simply trying to show how the Curly is similar to and different from the retrievers we know.

Physically, this breed is awesome: large, strong, durable. The English standard calls for adult males to run 25- to 27-inches at the withers and to weigh around 80 pounds. Many English Curlies exceed that standard considerably. In Australia and New Zealand, where hunters

expect their Curlies to tangle with swans that go 25 pounds and more, the breed dwarfs the English dog. Thus, overseas Curlies are comparable to our more substantial Chessies, and much larger than our Labradors and Goldens.

The relatively few American Curly breeders are sharply divided on what the "proper" size should be, some favoring the large type, others opting for males only about 50 pounds, still others breeding medium-sized dogs. While the duck and pheasant hunter can be well served by any of these, the goose hunter needs a big Curly. I realize that the "size of the fight in the dog" outweighs "the size of the dog in the fight," and all that; however, any well-bred field type Curly will come equipped with plenty of raw courage. The goose hunter should seek one with ample body to back it up.

The Curly, like his (rumored) American offspring, the Chesapeake Bay Retriever, possesses strength even beyond what his considerable size would suggest. Curly breeder Dick Guerin of Londonderry, New Hampshire told me that a big male of his entertains himself by diving down in the Guerins' pond to bring up sunken logs from the bottom. Powerful dogs.

The solid black or solid liver coat is the breed's greatest asset, even though misinformation about it has turned many away. This is not the loose, fluffy coat of the Poodle. It is not even the loose, hard coat of the Irish Water Spaniel. It is—if it is a "proper" Curly coat— hard and tightly curled against the dog's body. It may be oily or dry, depending on the dog's diet. Either way, it is waterproof, and (amazingly) burr-proof.

In water the Curly's coat protects far better than does the Golden's or the Flat-Coat's, significantly better than the Irish Water Spaniel's or the Labrador's, and about as well as the Chessy's. Curly breeder Kathy Tucker of Bellevue, Washington told me that her Curlies' skins are never wet, no matter how many retrieves they make, or

(Adapted from "The Curly-Coated Retriever," *Wildfowl*, February/March, 1987.)

37

how long it takes one of them to chase down a cripple. In the coldest, most miserable weather, her dogs act as if it were the first day of spring.

In the uplands the Curly's coat protects him from briars and brambles better than the coat of any other retriever breed. That tight, hard mass of curls withstands any cover less formidable than rolled barbed-wire. Warren Caldwell of Orisino, Idaho, hunts upland birds in the mountains with his Curlies. He assured me that there isn't a bramble patch in Idaho tough enough to deter one of his dogs if there is a bird to be flushed or retrieved from it.

The Curly's coat doesn't pick up burrs in the uplands the way Golden, Flat-Coat, and Irish Water Spaniel coats do. It snugs up against the skin too hard and tight to allow burrs to penetrate.

Dick Guerin hunts New Hampshire grouse with his Curlies and a Gordon Setter. "Afterwards," he said, "I have to spend about twenty minutes getting burrs from my setter, but my Curlies never pick any up."

Curly breeder Janean Marti of Cadott, Wisconsin hunts grouse and pheasants with her dogs. She said that her Curlies pick up very few burrs, and those few stay on the surface rather than working their way down under. Hair doesn't wrap around them the way it did on the setters she used to hunt. She simply plucks them off at the end of the day.

Curlies have great physical endurance. While not as fast and stylish as Labradors, they can go all day at the sensible pace they set. Warren Caldwell said that his never tire in the mountains of Idaho. They just plod along from morning to evening, uphill and down, until he calls them in.

My one-word description of the breed is, "persevering." They refuse to give up on a bird.

In September, 1986 I watched a yearling Curly, Whistler's Bay Hossa, owned by Jim Pougher of Logan, Utah, admirably demonstrate this quality in an HRC/UKC Hunt near Pueblo, Colorado. The dog got a difficult fall in a land single marking test. To make things worse, it was hot and still; no breeze to carry bird scent to the dog as he hunted the area of the fall. Hossa hunted for the bird an unbelievable length of time. He would stay in the area for about five minutes at a time, then leave to reassess his judgement of the area. Reconvinced every time, he returned for another five minutes or so. Time and again he came back to that area and hunted, until I lost track of how long he had been at it or how many times he had re-entered. Most dogs of most breeds would have given up and returned to their handlers, or at least looked back for a little help. Not this young Curly. The bird was there, and by George he was going to find it. It would be nice to be able to say that the youngster's perseverance finally paid off. It didn't. Eventually the judges, pressed for time for the other dogs, regretfully asked Jim to pick

Hossa up. However, the point here is perseverance, not success or failure. The dog never gave up. Never.

Curly-Coated Retrievers love water. The just-weaned pup reacts to his first water experience more like a Chessy than any other retriever breed: "Oh, boy, how long has this been going on? Whee! Get out of my way!"

Janean Marti told me about a young female that she boarded with a pro while she and her husband went on vacation. One day the dog escaped her run and headed straight for the nearest pond, jumped in, and swam happily around and around. The pro tried the usual trick to get the dog out: He tossed a dummy in the air so that it lit near him on land. The little female came out all right, but only long enough to snatch up the dummy, dodge the pro, and leap back into the pond. Several such attempts only littered the surface of the water with dummies. Finally the pro rowed out, tossed a dummy so it fell right next to the boat, and grabbed the gleeful Curly by the scruff of her neck when she came alongside after it.

The Curly learns quickly, especially from his own experience. He will figure out how to deal with river currents after only a couple of exposures. He masters wind, cover, and terrain variations with equal facility, and he learns faster than most breeds where birds are apt to be.

This canine cunning, combined with his legendary perseverance, is not an unmixed blessing. To a novice the Curly may often appear stubborn, but he is just lost in his own world, oblivious to the handler's commands.

Curlies love water, too. (Photo by Alan Coman, courtesy Kathy Tucker.)

Working with a Curly may seem at times like working with a Chesapeake, but there is an important underlying difference: When a Curly ignores a command, it will normally be because he is absorbed in his own thoughts; whereas the Chessy is more apt to be negotiating a larger role for himself in the trainer/trainee script. Get the Curly's attention, and he will readily obey. With the Chessy, you may have to do some additional convincing even after you have cleaned out his ears.

The typical Curly develops very slowly, physically and mentally—more so than any other retriever breed. Few Curlies will be completely mature by age two, and many take until age four. Their bones seem to grow faster than their muscles and tendons, which makes them appear awkward and gangly for a long time. Mentally and emotionally, some Curlies are extremely slow to become ready for serious training—thus, many good prospects are washed out before they can be realistically evaluated.

At home the Curly is a serious, unassuming, one-family dog. Definitely not the tail-wagging, hail-fellow-well-met Golden, his hospitality for strangers falls somewhere between that of the suspicious Irish Water Spaniel and that of the protective Chessy. Quietly undemonstrative with his own people, he is aloof with visitors, and some Curlies (not all) can be formidable watchdogs.

Janean Marti said hers are good watchdogs. Once a neighbor who tried to enter the Marti backyard from the woods was firmly turned away by Janean's two Curlies. The dogs showed no aggressiveness; didn't chase the neighbor back into the woods. They simply stood their ground in the backyard, growled convincingly, and showed their surgical equipment. Janean said this neighbor has never had any trouble entering from the front.

Training a Curly can be anything from the easiest job you ever undertook to the most frustrating, depending on what you expect. The breed was developed to do certain things naturally, and as long as you stay within those limits, training is a snap. However, when you try to improve on nature, you face a tough job.

The Curly retrieves naturally on land and in water, and he loves to hunt and flush upland game. English gamekeepers (and poachers, too, for that matter), who had little time for dog training, developed the breed to do these things naturally. If you use a Curly as the gamekeepers always have, relying more on the dog's instincts than formal training, you will be delighted with his performance most of the time.

The English Magnum. Ch. Charwin Scirocco CD WCX SD, owned by Kathy Tucker. (Photo by Kathy Tucker.)

However, if you try to impose our American field trial discipline, you face a major struggle every day. They take to this kind of rote drilling far less graciously than a Labrador or Golden, even somewhat less so than the Chessy (which also started as a natural dog, but now has many decades of field trial breeding behind it). Curlies are still naturals, "untainted" by field trial formalities.

For example, blind retrieve training and the control it demands violates everything that has been bred into him. Such training, therefore, guarantees a battle of wills that the trainer will surely give up on before the dog does. A Curly relies on his in-bred "hunt," and will only slowly and grudgingly yield his own opinion of where an unseen bird came down to that of his whistle-tooting, arm-waving owner. Even after the Curly has been thoroughly drilled in lining, stopping, and casting, he will probably revert to type when the chips are down, and turn his handler off. He becomes so absorbed in his own instincts that he just doesn't hear the whistle.

That is the price one pays for a dog with such great perseverance and determination.

However, if you stay within the limits his nature dictates, you will find the Curly an outstanding performer. In these days when hunting success or failure frequently depends on the retrieving of one or two birds, it is nice to have a dog around that will doggedly pursue that crippled duck that plunged into the heavy tules, or that wing-tipped goose that took off running for the next county.

The recent growth in American goose populations could bring this hardy English retriever his first real opportunity in this country. A well-bred Curly puppy has almost the same probability of growing up to be a successful gooser as has the well-bred Chesapeake Bay Retriever—and a substantially greater probability than any other retriever breed. The Curly is big, strong, tough-bodied, and confident, like the Chessy. True, the Bay dog carries a bit more of each of these traits, but just a bit.

However, the Curly pup has a greater probability of becoming an exceptional upland game dog than has the Chessy pup. Here the breed compares favorably with the Labrador. Labs may be faster workers, but the Curly's bullet-proof coat can withstand nastier cover, and the Curly's slower pace is more comfortable, requiring less handler control and whistle-tooting. Besides, at their pace, they can go all day.

If a reasonable number of these animals could be given a fair chance in this country, they could catch on and develop a following similar to that of the Chesapeake (the American magnum wildfowler). Neither will rival the popularity of the Labrador or Golden, just as the 10-gauge will never rival the popularity of the 12.

That doesn't mean a big 10 isn't nice to have in the blind when geese are coming in. Ditto for the Curly-Coated Retriever.

THE IRISH WATER SPANIEL: AN IRISHMAN'S IRISHMAN

Shakespeare's line, "What's in a name? A rose by any other name would smell as sweet," may apply to roses, Juliets, and the better English gins. It may even apply to some breeds of sporting dogs. For example, the misnamed Labrador doesn't let the fact that he is actually from Newfoundland interfere with his work. However, there are limits that even Shakespeare's persuasive phrasing cannot breach.

Take the Irish Water Spaniel. If you will just meditate on the name, you will understand the breed. The name tells all. This is a spaniel, bred for water work, by the Irish.

Irish, to be sure; Irish, above all. However, first let's run through the impact of the other two words, and then come back to Irish.

Physically, the Irish Water Spaniel (IWS) is a substantial dog by spaniel standards. With the males standing 23- to 25-inches at the withers and weighing 65- to 75-pounds, the IWS dwarfs the better-known spaniels like the Brittany, the Springer, and the Cocker. The IWS needs plenty of size to do the job he was designed for: retrieve ducks and geese from rough, cold water.

Like most spaniel breeds, the IWS trains up easily, at least in the work for which they were specifically bred. They are people-oriented, eager to please, warm and affectionate. The normal, well-adjusted IWS—like the normal, well-adjusted Springer or Brittany—delights in pleasing the boss, so if the boss is clever enough to communicate what he wants, the IWS will happily do it, and then wag all over expecting the approval that means so much to every spaniel. Praise and appreciation, profusely expressed through kind words and petting, are the primary

motivators for the IWS. It is a wise boss who uses them often, even when he doesn't feel like it.

Being a spaniel, the IWS tends toward softness and sensitivity. He needs a training program that is predominantly positive, one in which correction and punishment remain in the background as a last resort. When the trainer experiences one of "those days" with his Irisher, he will promote the team's long-term success more by stopping to try again another day than by persisting in futile corrections. Of course, he should remember that the IWS, like all spaniels, learns quickly how to play on the sympathy of a too tender-hearted trainer and get his way through an outstanding dramatic performance in which the dog assumes the role of an abused canine that simply cannot grasp what he is doing wrong. For this reason, the wise trainer will force the issue before terminating any training session that has gone awry. This prevents the IWS from out-maneuvering him with his "poor, poor me" act.

Again, being a spaniel, the breed boasts an outstanding nose, which enables him to wind a downed bird from an unbelievable distance. Here the IWS rivals the Golden and the Flat-Coat, and surpasses the other retriever breeds.

Every discussion of the breed leads quickly to concern about its curly locks and the problems associated with them. Even hunters who think nothing of spending a few minutes at the end of the day digging burrs from a Golden view the IWS coat with suspicion. Those who have never hunted any long-haired breed tend to dismiss any thought of trying an Irisher as soon as they see all that hair. Since it constitutes such a major concern, let's talk about that mass of curls.

Like most retrievers, the IWS sports a double coat. He has a dense wooly undercoat that keeps him warm in cold weather; this is the coat he sheds every spring. Then, there is the liver-colored curly outercoat which looks like

(Adapted from 'The Irish Water Spaniel," *Gun Dog*, September/October, 1986; and "The Irish Water Spaniel," *Wildfowl*, August/September, 1987.)

The Irish Water Spaniel's name tells all. (Photo by Elissa Kirkegard.)

that of a Poodle. There is a significant difference, for the Poodle has a soft and absorbant coat whereas the Irisher has a harsh, springy, slightly oily coat that sheds water and protects the dog from brambles. While the oil is not sufficient to be picked up by even the most sensitive human olfactory nerves, it is sufficient to prevent the dog from becoming waterlogged in the ordinary practice of his profession. On the average—and granting that there are exceptions—the IWS coat does a better job than that of the Golden or Flat-Coat, but it falls short of the Labrador's, considerably behind the Curly-Coat's, and light-years to the rear of the Chesapeake's magnificent coat.

How much care does the IWS coat require? Well, breed authority Elissa Kirkegard of Doylestown, Pennsylvania, recommends that at a minimum the coat be combed out and trimmed twice a year: once just before hunting season, and again in the spring when the dog sheds his undercoat. Beyond that, the owner need only remove any burrs the dog picks up in training and hunting. Of course, every Irisher loves the camaraderie of being groomed, and many owners come to enjoy this quiet communal time so much that they comb and brush once a week. Elissa admits that she grooms her IWS a lot more than the minimum she recommends.

Hair care for the Irish, then, runs about the same as it does for any long-coated hunting dog. However, the consequences of neglect are more serious for this breed. The outer and undercoats become one tangled mass, while the outercoat may also begin to "cord," leaving long braids hanging everywhere. A dog in this condition has difficulty moving, and he suffers more from skin disease and parasites.

However, you shouldn't look on the IWS as simply a support system for his admittedly demanding double coat. He is a lot of spaniel, a lot of retriever, and especially a lot of water dog.

While he can do outstanding work in the uplands, the Irisher belongs beside a duck hunter. As a matter of fact, his coat doesn't create a problem as long as he works in the water, which is the environment for which he was developed. Only when he asks his IWS to "moonlight" in the uplands does the owner have to prick his fingers pulling burrs from the animal's curly locks. In the water that coat is all pluses.

The IWS loves water; swims strongly for as long as necessary. Not as fast in the water as the Labrador, the Irisher has the endurance of the Chesapeake. Strong, methodical, persistent, tireless, he traces back to dogs that

42

retrieved ducks when there were seemingly limitless ducks to be retrieved.

Like all retriever breeds and spaniels, the IWS is a natural retriever. Young pups, barely big enough to waddle, delight in carrying anything they can get in their mouths.

The Irisher is a pleasure to have in a duckblind. He will sit quietly at your side until you send him after a downed bird. He will not demand constant attention, nor dance and prance endlessly, as do some high-strung retrievers. The IWS is all serenity until there is work to do. He is content to sit by your side and watch the sky with you. Oh, an occasional pat on the shoulder or a kind word pleases him, but he can get by without them if you are off in another world. Like two good friends, you and your IWS can enjoy each other even when nothing is said and nothing is happening.

The third, and most important element in the breed's character is that it was developed in Ireland. In fact, my one-word description for the breed is "Irish." He is everything that word connotes.

While there are occasional references to Irish Water Spaniels clear back to the first century A.D.—and those who equate antiquity with goodness make much of these—the breed's real history began in Dublin around 1850 when a "foin auld gentleman" named Justin McCarthy bred dogs of the same conformation we see today. With that sort of start in life, the Irish Water Spaniel certainly must carry strong indications in his character that he was developed in the land of saints, scholars, leprechauns, and tough, courageous Micks. And that he does; that he does.

One of the strongest traits of the Irish people is their love of the land; their love of home. Margaret Mitchell dramatized this magnificently in *Gone With the Wind.* Remember how early in the book Gerald O'Hara told his mocking daughter, Scarlett, that she would always love the family plantation, Tara, that her roots were in Tara's land? Remember, too, how as she matured, Scarlett developed this Irish trait in spite of herself—to the point that she could never remain away from Tara for long, and always returned there when she had a real problem to work out? Scarlett O'Hara was many things, but most of all she was Irish.

The Irish Water Spaniel loves his home and family, too. This attachment is the basis for the breed's character, and no one will ever understand the breed until he understands this very Irish trait.

The IWS tends to be a one-family dog rather than a one-man dog. He adopts the entire clan—and all the clan's property—as his own, and he is happiest on his own sod with his own people. He is not inclined to wander, probably wouldn't even go hunting with a stranger if given a choice. This characteristic makes it highly advisable that a family member do the training of the resident IWS. Being trained by a family member is a joy, but it is a sad-hearted misery when done by strangers away from home.

The Irish Water Spaniel will protect his own, too, although not as aggressively as some breeds. When no family member is present, there is little chance that a stranger will lay shoe leather on the family plot. Slow to bite, the IWS stands his ground menacingly, and will oblige any challenger that insists on intrusion.

Even when welcomed by the family, a stranger cannot count on too much initial warmth from the Irish Water Spaniel. The understanding visitor will ignore the animal and allow him to make his own judgement in his own time, trusting to the dog's kindly heart to properly measure the visitor's good intentions. Such a stranger will shortly feel the touch of a wet nose on his hand, a sure sign of IWS acceptance. On the other hand, the pushy visitor will meet resolute aloofness until he gives up his over-eager attempts to make up with the dog and lets the dog do things in his own time and manner.

The breed has its typically Irish "scholarly" side, too. Pat Brenner, breeder/trainer in Wisconsin, told me that her experience indicates that the IWS learns almost anything—good or bad—with fewer repetitions than the other retriever breeds. This means that a trainer can condition a typical IWS with less drill, drill, drill, which is wonderful for the average owner/trainer with limited time. However, the IWS picks up the errors and mistakes with fewer repetitions, too, so care is required. Pat said that whatever is learned by the IWS is tatooed permanently in his brain very quickly. If the owner accidentally teaches the wrong thing, retraining will be a nightmare. Thus, the IWS owner should take great care to get it right the first time.

The breed has a bit of the leprechaun in it, too. For example, the IWS has a unique movement which is difficult to describe. They are bouncy, seeming to fly sometimes. The title of the English breed book by Nick Water, *A Bundle of Rags in a Cyclone,* comes as close as anything to describing their acrobatic way of getting from one place to another. Even when driving hard after a downed bird, the typical Irisher has a lot of up-and-down in his movement, giving his retrieving style a jauntiness found in no other breed.

With his own people the IWS will play the frolicsome clown, sometimes the practical joker that will hide this or that, or try to cajole his way out of serious training. His "bundle of rags in a cyclone" movement heightens the humor of this prankishness, sometimes allowing him to turn work time to play time, even in the most regimented households. The IWS has a charming way of ending the training session by pretending not to understand while he cons you into lightening up on him. You know the situation: You feel that with just one more repetition he will have something down just right; you try him one more time and everything falls apart. If you are not wise to his tactic, you will conclude that you did something different this time to confuse him. The knowing owner will quickly determine whether the IWS is playing games or is really having problems. If the former, which is more likely for this bright animal, said owner will force the issue and then quit for the day. That is a win-win solution that the Irisher can understand.

The IWS is a tough, courageous Mick, too. With other dogs, the Irisher (at least those of the male persuasion) love a free-swinging brawl, especially if the participants are all Irish Water Spaniels: the worthiest of opponents. They are jealous and short-tempered with each other, and should not be kenneled together. Put a bunch of them in close quarters and surely one will sing out that line from the "Clancy Lowered the Boom" song that goes: "Let's have some fun—I think I'll start a fight!"

Which brings us to another Irish trait found in the IWS as a hunter: courage, both physical and moral. While his double coat offers reasonable protection from cold water, it won't prevent all discomfort on really bad days. Even so, the IWS will sit by the blind, perhaps shivering occasionally, and never hesitate to hit the water when sent after a downed bird. After a long chase, it may be a thoroughly soggy Irisher that delivers a lively cripple to the blind inhabitants, and the north wind may cause the dog's teeth to chatter as little icicles form on his curls. Still, give him a moment to shake off and he will happily throw himself back into the icy surf for another chase. Because of this courage, the owner should be sure the dog is reasonably comfortable between retrieves—given plenty of time to shake off, and placed out of the wind when it blows cold and strong.

There you have the Irish Water Spaniel. A wonderful waterfowl retriever that can also do journeyman duties in the upland; a frolicsome, prankish, totally unpredictable clown that will dote on you, protect you and yours, devote his life to you, and yet never let you feel that he is completely trained. A dog that will force you to do more barbering and grooming than you really want to, but one that will make that grooming time so much fun that you will enjoy it in spite of yourself. A dog for which the name says everything: Irish. Water. Spaniel.

Is this the dog for you? If you are primarily a waterfowler, that's a plus. If you like the spaniel way of doing things, so much the better. However, perhaps the real issue here is how do you feel about the Irish people? Believe me, this dog is all Irish, with all the virtues and vices of that nationality. If you like the Irish, you will get along fine with the Irish Water Spaniel.

The IWS coat is good protection in water. (Photo by Elissa Kirkegard.)

Here is a good look at the IWS coat. (Photo by Elissa Kirkegard.)

Keegan, Melissa Fulsom's IWS, simply couldn't be excluded from her wedding. Family breed, indeed! (Photo by Jerry Wurz.)

10

THE AMERICAN WATER SPANIEL: YANKEE DOODLE DANDY

The American Water Spaniel (AWS) is as American as George M. Cohan, and just as capable of "doing it all" in his particular line of work.

Primarily a marvelous little all-weather ducker, the AWS can also bust the nastiest cover in the uplands to flush and retrieve birds for the boss. The dog's small size and placid temperament make him ideal in a duck skiff, where he can slip into and out of the water without upsetting or soaking the skipper. His methodical thoroughness in the uplands makes him a delightful companion for the gunner over thirty-five years of age.

Developed in the last century in the Great Lakes region, and now the State Dog of Wisconsin, this native breed possesses so many talents that the parent club, American Water Spaniel Club of America (AWSCA), cannot decide whether to seek AKC classification as a retriever or as a flushing spaniel. AKC requires classification as one or the other before it will allow the AWS to participate in field trials and hunting tests. While the AWS needs the exposure these activities would give it among dog-loving hunters, the choice of either "retriever-dom" or "spaniel-dom" would threaten the long-term dual talents of the breed. The leadership of AWSCA is split three ways: Some want to class the breed as a retriever and risk allowing its spaniel talents to atrophy; others want to class the breed as a spaniel and take a corresponding risk with its waterfowling abilities; still others—those who maintain control as long as neither of the other two groups establishes majority support—prefer to leave the breed unclassified and continue to run their own unique combination tests.

The AKC, which has long recognized the breed within its sporting group, could resolve this problem by allowing the breed dual classification, thereby giving the AWS the opportunity to run in both retriever and spaniel trials and tests. However, the smart money is running heavily against such an AKC accommodation.

The breed can enter the retriever tests sponsored by both the Hunting Retriever Club (HRC), which is affiliated with the United Kennel Club (UKC), and the North American Hunting Retriever Association, which has no registry affiliation.

Okay, let's look at this spunky little Yankee water dog that has more talents than one AKC classification can encompass.

A bantam-weight by retriever standards, he weighs only about 40 pounds and stands some 18 inches at the withers. This small stature, more that of a big Cocker or small Springer, clearly says "spaniel." However, his long tail says "waterfowler." I gained great respect for the usefulness of a long tail on any quadruped with all four feet off the ground one day when I watched a tail-less squirrel struggle cautiously through the trees in our backyard while his fully-tailed buddies did aerial acrobatics around him.

The AWS coat also says "waterfowler," and runs the entire retriever spectrum. It can be anything from the flat, harsh, slightly wavy coat of the Chesapeake to the tight, hard curls of the Curly-Coated Retriever. The less curl there is, the more dense the undercoat. Most American Water Spaniels have coats somewhere in the middle, similar to that of the Irish Water Spaniel. Regardless of coat type, the outercoat is relatively short, only about one-half inch longer than that of the Labrador.

This coat protects the dog quite well in the normally cold water of the upper Midwest, its region of origin. It also protects him from briars and brambles in the uplands. However, it does pick up burrs, and they do work their way into the undercoat, where they are a real challenge to the owner. While there is no way to avoid the chore of pulling burrs at the end of the day—before cleaning

(Adapted from "The American Water Spaniel," *Wildfowl*, April/May, 1987.)

Sargent Barney Good Times, Vaughn Brockman's all-time favorite American Water Spaniel.

the birds, your gun, and your aching anatomy—most AWS owners have found ways to minimize the task. Sharon Beaupre of Cambridge, Minnesota, lightly trims her dog's coat before opening day—not enough to expose the dog to the elements, but just enough to make him less of a burr-magnet. Dr. Gary Forshee of Bonner Springs, Kansas, puts a light coat of cheap hair oil ("The cheaper and greasier the better," he says) on his AWS so the burrs don't twist into the undercoat. This lubrication also facilitates their removal.

The character of the AWS is pure American. In fact, my one-word description of the breed is: "opportunistic."

Perhaps the most distinctive AWS quality is their peculiarly American intelligence. Call them clever, crafty, or whatever, they can *carpe diem* (capture the day) better than any dog that walks, swims, and barks.

For example, in the early days of the heartworm problem, Tom Olson of Milaca, Minnesota, began giving his AWS daily carricide pills. The dog accepted each one, feigned chewing until Tom turned away, and then hid the pill behind an out-of-the-way chair. One day Tom found about thirty pills back there, and realized he had been outsmarted.

Vaughn Brockman of Menomonie, Wisconsin, had an AWS, Sargent Barney Good Times, back in the 1960s that became a legend among Vaughn's hunting and non-hunting friends for his craftiness. In an effort to control Barney's range in the uplands, Vaughn bought an electronic collar, one of those early models that only worked when the dog was grounded. The dealer assured Vaughn that he could solve the problem forever with no more than

three jolts. Clearly, he had no experience with the AWS in general and Barney in particular. Within the first three jolts, Barney realized that the discomfort went away when he jumped, and also when he put a lot of distance between himself and the boss. Vaughn still laughs when he tells of watching Barney make long kangaroo leaps, one after another, as he hustled out of the transmitter's range. That was exactly the opposite of what Vaughn had in mind, and therefore precisely what Barney had to do to win.

AWS's are possessive, so they make excellent watchdogs for those who allow this trait to develop. However, if the owner shows that he disapproves of that kind of behavior, the average AWS will desist.

A very personal dog, the AWS becomes attached to one family and especially to one member of that family. He focuses his life on that one person, bonds only with him/her, and manipulates the other family members as required. For this reason, that one person should train the dog. The AWS does not respond well to professional training, unless the pro can establish a strong bond with the animal first—which takes time and therefore costs money.

As a youngster Sargent Barney Good Times went to a pro, from whom he learned plenty in his own crafty way. From the first day, Barney steadfastly refused to acknowledge the pro's existence, much less accept his training. After three weeks of futility, the pro called and told Vaughn to come and get his worthless dog. When Vaughn arrived, the pro gave him a demonstration with Barney. However, instead of refusing to work, Barney did everything right! Reluctantly, the pro agreed to keep the dog for another try. Three weeks later, he called Vaughn again and told him that all Barney would do was sit and watch the other dogs work. When Vaughn picked Barney up, this time without a demonstration, the pro told him that he hoped that he would never see another AWS in his life. During the following hunting season, Vaughn found that Barney had learned plenty just sitting and watching the other dog work.

"In fact," Vaughn chuckles, "Barney hunted like a fully trained dog ever after!"

Pro Tom Dokken of Northfield, Minnesota, has trained many AWS's over the past few years, so he has some interesting insights into the breed's personality. He says they mature more slowly than Labradors, and learn more slowly, too. Tom takes a typical Lab through his basic program in three months, but has to spend four or five months cajoling a typical AWS through it. He feels that he succeeds more frequently with AWS's that have been well socialized at home before he gets them; that he bonds more easily with such dogs. Tom prefers starting an AWS at about five months old, when the dog is still quite malleable.

The AWS is physically tough, durable, and healthy. Dr. Gary Forshee, who has been training and hunting them for twelve years, told me he has yet to spend a buck at his vet's for anything but elective procedures and repair of hunting injuries. None of his AWS's has ever come down with any of the many current canine maladies. Douglas Doyle of Stanfordville, New York, told me that his vet calls the AWS the toughest breed he has ever treated.

Mentally tough, too, the AWS has enough aggressiveness for an occasional crippled honker. While the goose hunting specialist needs a bigger retriever, the catch-as-catch-can hunter who shoots an occasional goose can depend on an AWS to bring it in to him somehow. Vaughn Brockman once tried unsuccessfully to keep a nine-month-old female puppy from going after a bluffing and blustering crippled Greater Canada. The youngster broke and charged the puffed-up, hissing honker, hitting it full-tilt in the chest. This bowled the bird over and knocked it senseless, making it easy for the little dog to grab its neck and drag it back. Driving through a bird and then picking it up on the way back seems to be a trait more common in American dogs. I have seen Chessies do this often, but I can't remember ever seeing any other retriever breed do it.

Douglas Doyle, who hunts a little of everything with his AWS's, told me that his dogs retrieve about a half-dozen geese a year. I asked if they are all stone-dead. "Are *yours* all stone-dead?" he answered. Good point.

The breed is tough in other ways, too. One of Douglas Doyle's dogs was sucked into a culvert full of rushing water while retrieving a duck in a flooded field with a road through it. The dog thrashed his way out on the other side with the duck still in his mouth, and didn't hesitate to leap back into the water the next time Douglas shot a bird.

For all his mental and physical toughness, the AWS has a strong sense of fair play, which the smart owner will never violate. In this, the breed resembles two other American breeds with which I am familiar: the Chesapeake Bay Retriever and the Boston Terrier.

The AWS will accept punishment in training, as long as he understands what he did to deserve it. However, he won't put up with mistreatment, for it violates his sense of fair play. If the trainer establishes proper rapport with the AWS and takes the time to lead him through the training, punishment will seldom be needed. The AWS really wants to please that one human with whom he is bonded.

If the trainer, even that special person, abuses the AWS by too severe punishment or incomprehensible punishment or even excessive neglect, the dog will quit, refuse to work, and turn him off. A surprisingly few repetitions will convert this into a permanent condition, creating a dog that may never trust another human being: a canine robot that goes through the motions of living with none of the spaniel merriment.

The AWS may use his opportunistic intelligence to deal with mild punishment he feels is unjustified. For example, in one family the husband handled all canine corrections. Whenever the dog felt justice had not been properly served on a specific occasion, he would sneak into the bedroom, pull the husband's pillow—never the wife's—off the bed, and lift his leg on it. The man could hardly ignore such eloquent complaints, so he and the dog gradually negotiated a mutually acceptable code of "canine criminal law."

The AWS will figure ways to deal with every person in the household, especially those who dislike dogs. Years ago in Wisconsin there was an AWS-owning parish priest whose assistant didn't share his enthusiasm for dogs. The AWS sensed and resented this attitude, or course, so he haughtily ignored the offending assistant. However, on occasion he would take revenge by keeping this priest awake at night by waiting quietly outside the assistant's bedroom window until about five minutes after the light went out. Then, the dog would yodel softly, just loud enough to be heard in the one room. When the light came back on, the dog would be quiet again, waiting until about five minutes after it went out again before resuming his serenade. His timing assured that the priest would just get to sleep each time before being waked up again. The dog would repeat this for several hours. Ultimately, the assistant was transferred to another parish—and the AWS probably took his departure as a "personal" triumph, as proof of who really ran the parish.

The breed does have a tendency to yodel. The one in the story above used to join his owner in singing High Mass on Sundays—from the safety of the rectory window.

The AWS is a tough little dog. (Photo by Vaughn Brockman.)

The coat and tail indicate the AWS was designed for water work. (Photo by Vaughn Brockman.)

Yodeling becomes an operatic art form with some AWS's. A true Caruso of the breed sits down, points his muzzle to the heavens, opens his jaw, closes his lips until his mouth is a small round hole, and then moans softly. In an urban setting, such unearthly sounds in the middle of the night can reduce neighborly harmony to a dangerously low level. However, the AWS will accept early training in "Hush!", thereby never developing his full operatic range.

Many American Water Spaniels "grin." This looks like a snarl, for the dog curls his lip up, uncovering his teeth. However, when grinning he also wags and dances all over, showing his delight at seeing a family member or at the prospect of going hunting. The dog's total demeanor shows that he is grinning, not snarling. Many Chesapeakes show happiness this way, too.

The AWS is a delightful dog, a character if you will. However, he has never regained his pre-World War II popularity, even in the upper Midwest. Since the end of the Big One, highly publicized imports have dominated the American hunting dog scene to the detriment of our home-breds, especially the American Water Spaniel. Too bad, for no other breed can do so many things the American hunter needs done—which is understandable, for the breed was developed right here long before we started adapting British and European breeds to our needs.

This may change in the near future. Many modern American hunters live in areas which don't allow more than one dog, or in dwellings that favor the smaller dog: apartments, condos, urban and suburban houses with tiny yards. The AWS fits into any of these environments, in fact into any environment suitable for human habitation. Besides, the AWS will hunt anything a feather-chaser can stuff in his game bag. Some even use them for rabbits.

Douglas Doyle summed it up like this: "I can hunt everything I want to hunt in my area (New York) with an American Water Spaniel, and do it on less dog food."

While the American Water Spaniel is certainly a do-it-all dog that is cheap to keep, he is so much more. A delight around the house, he has the charming ability to smile at his owner and communicate, if not say, George M. Cohan's immortal line: "My mother thanks you. My father thanks you. My sister thanks you. And I thank you!"

11

THE NOVA SCOTIA DUCK TOLLING RETRIEVER: THE DOG BEHIND ALL THAT NAME

This is a wonderful breed that has suffered too long from an overdose of its own name. The name is certainly descriptive, and quite accurate in telling where the dog originated and what its major functions have historically been. The breed's name is practically its resume, which may seem like a good idea at first. The trouble is, it's so easy to get caught up in the romance of the "tolling" legend—frolicking foxes luring rafted waterfowl to shore, Indians doing the same thing with a fox hide on a rope between two blinds, and the breed of dogs that was specifically developed to attract or "toll" ducks and geese to shore for the hunter—that very little has been written about the dog himself: his personality and his temperament, as distinct from his function.

It is time to change that. It is time to look first at the intriguing personality and hardy character of the Toller and only after these have been properly treated, to chant again the tolling legend.

Physically, the Toller looks like a cross between the gorgeous Golden Retriever and the equally attractive red fox. This may sound strange—and it has nothing to do with the dog's actual ancestry—but it is a good short description for those not familiar with the breed.

The males stand about 20 inches at the withers (top of shoulders) and weigh 45- to 50-pounds. As with all breeds, the females average a little shorter and lighter. That makes them the second smallest of the eight retriever breeds, only slightly larger than the American Water Spaniel.

The Toller has the true retriever double coat, with a wooly undercoat for warmth, and a long, somewhat silky outercoat for water- and weather-proofing. The outercoat is straight, slightly shorter and harsher than that of the Golden Retriever. The Toller color range approximates that of the Golden, varying from blonde to dark shades only slightly lighter than the Irish Setter's mahogany. The Toller may have white on the feet, chest, face, and tail,

and this is very attractive. A white tip on the merry Toller tail is especially pleasing.

The Toller's face and tail resemble those of the red fox rather than the Golden Retriever. The face is "tight"—somewhat pointed—and the tail is very bushy.

The Toller's movement is quite distinctive: merry, animated, saucy. While this bounciness is essential to the tolling function, as I will explain later, it is also part of the breed's Scottish heritage. In fact, you can almost hear bagpipes as you watch a Toller's jaunty way of coming and going.

Yes, they are "Canadians of Scottish extraction," like so many of the people of Nova Scotia. Before the French and Indian War, that area of eastern Canada was "Acadia," occupied by the French. After the war, the English crown drove the French out and encouraged thousands of hardy Scots to emigrate there. Thus, the name was changed to Nova Scotia (New Scotland). Many of the French Acadians migrated to Louisiana, where "Acadian" was slurred into "Cajun," a name their descendants cherish to this day. There has been speculation that the French may have had something to do with the development of the Toller, but if that were true, why isn't the breed native to Louisiana as well as Nova Scotia? No, it is as sure as anything in canine history can be that this is a Nova Scotian breed developed by the Scots who settled there.

My one-word description of the breed is, "hardy."

The temperament of the Toller reflects the Scottish influence: clannish, sociable, docile, animated, stubborn, eager to please, tough, sensitive, aloof, and affectionate. While this may seem to be a string of contradictions, the key to all of them can be found in the first of that list of adjectives: clannish. The Toller, like a typical Scot, is one thing to those within his own clan, and something quite different to outsiders. The Scots have been known throughout their history for their extremes of devotion to

49

clan and coldness toward outsiders. It would be surprising if the Tollers didn't take on these same traits through the breed's long association with these people.

Within his clan—which includes everyone, related or not, that the dog accepts as one of his people—the Toller is a cooperative joy. He is sociable, eager to please, sensitive, affectionate, and either docile or animated as the situation requires. For his one special person within that clan, he is almost a mind reader, and certainly a mirror of the boss's changing moods.

To those outside his clan, the Toller is aloof, and can become stubborn and tough if the need arises. While not inclined to bite, the Toller makes a good watchdog because of his innate suspiciousness toward strangers. He will definitely bark and let his owner know something is amiss, and if pressed, he will stand his ground with typical Scottish staunchness.

This clannishness has significant implications with regard to his training, whether for hunting, obedience trials, or just good citizenship around the homestead. Professional trainers frequently find the breed difficult to work with, while owners normally find them very easy. The difference, of course, is in the animal's differing attitudes toward the two trainers. He loves his owner, so will do anything he even suspects might please that person; he is suspicious of the pro, so will do nothing the pro wants him to do (and he can be quite hardheaded about it, too). Obviously, the secret to training a Toller lies in establishing and maintaining rapport with the dog. Even the owner can bring out the animal's Scottish stubborn-

ness by being too heavy-handed, too sparing with praise and petting, or even by rushing things too much. The toller wants to be a participating member of the training team, not a flunky; a retriever, but not a "gofer." He flourishes in an atmosphere of mutual respect, appreciation, and affection. Share these with him and he will do anything for you. Withhold them and he will do nothing for you. In fact, he may use his Scottish wit to really "stick it to you" now and then.

The Canadian Kennel Club (CKC) first recognized the breed in 1945, and then had to almost start over again in 1959 because the Tollers had nearly died out. In America, the UKC recognizes the breed, but the AKC has not yet come around. The breed has never been extremely popular, even in its native Nova Scotia, perhaps largely due to its resume-like name, but in recent years the number of Tollers registered in Canada has been increasing rather rapidly. It is still a very rare breed in the United States which is unfortunate, for the toller can fit beautifully into today's typical American urban lifestyle.

Like all retriever breeds, the Toller has a strong retrieving instinct—a mania for fetching, really—and a love for water that is hard for many new owners to understand. The Toller is nicely configured for the modern one-dog waterfowl and upland game hunter, in that the dog is small enough to live in an apartment, docile enough to sit quietly by the blind for those long periods of inactivity, hardy enough to plunge into the coldest water, and energetic enough to wiggle through the thickest of briars and brambles all day in the uplands.

The Toller is an attractive dog that resembles the Golden Retriever. Ch. Ardunacres Country Quincey. (Photo by Arline MacDonald, Ardunacres Kennel.

Tollers may have white touches in their orange coats. (Photo by Arline MacDonald, Ardunacres Kennel.)

Okay, now for the breed's name, and some of the romantic legends associated with it.

The word *toll,* which is from the middle English word *tollen,* means to attract, and it has been used primarily to describe various ways to attract waterfowl. For example, many years ago, when live decoys were legal for duck hunting, they were called ''tollers.''

Foxes have always had their own way of tolling ''rafted'' ducks (large flocks sitting together in the middle of a lake) on those days when a fresh duck dinner appeals to them. They work in pairs. One fox lies quietly at the water's edge, while the other prances around, sometimes tossing a stick in the air and jumping to catch it. For reasons no one really understands, this attracts the wariest of ducks and geese. Even black ducks have difficulty keeping their distance. The antics of the gamboling fox seem to mesmerize waterfowl. Eventually, one of the unsuspecting birds swims within pouncing distance of the other fox (the one lying in ambush), and voila! dinner for two.

Ancient Indians imitated this technique, using a fox hide which they pulled and jiggled back and forth between two blinds on a rope. It has been suggested that Indians even trained foxes or dogs to do some form of tolling, and that that is where Nova Scotians got the idea for the Toller breed.

Regardless of where they discovered the concept, they did indeed develop a dog that can be easily trained to do

a form of tolling. While no one is certain what dogs were used to create the Toller, it is apparent that the intent was to develop a breed that closely resembled the legendary Reynard—in general conformation, color, markings, and animation. However, the Toller is significantly larger than the red fox for two reasons: greater visibility while tolling, and adequate size for its retrieving function.

There is no question that the breed can successfully toll ducks in a manner similar to the one used by the foxes, for the breed is still doing it today in the proper surroundings, especially in its native Nova Scotia. The Toller's technique is not identical to that of the fox from the human point of view, but the ducks and geese cannot tell the difference. They do it like this:

The hunter sets up several blinds, or ''ambushes,'' around a big lake, positioning each one near the shore where the water is deep and free from weeds and trees— rafted ducks will more readily swim into such places. On the day of the hunt, the hunter scouts the lake to see where the ducks are rafted up, and then hides in the closest ambush. He tosses a stick down to the water's edge for his dog to retrieve. The Toller romps out merrily, picks up the stick, and bounces back to the ambush. Although the dog is merely doing an ordinary retrieve, to the ducks his movement resembles that of the gamboling fox. That's why Tollers were bred to have such a stylish way of getting from one place to another. A flashy white tip on the

51

dog's tail is very desirable, both because it is highly visible from a great distance, and because it adds to the animation of the dog's movement. The Toller retrieving the stick along the shoreline attracts the ducks and they start swimming toward shore. As long as they continue coming in, the hunter and dog remain quietly in the ambush; if the birds hesitate, the hunter tosses the stick for another retrieve; and so on until the birds are within range. Then the hunter flushes the ducks and shoots; if he brings down a bird, the Toller leaps into the lake and retrieves it.

This is much easier than traditional duck hunting over decoys. First off, it works on the nicest of days, whereas regular hunting is best in the worst possible weather. Further, the hunter doesn't have to get up in the middle of the night, for he must wait until the birds have come back from feeding in the morning and rafted up. He doesn't even have to lug, put out, and pick up dozens of decoys, for his dog will toll the birds. Nor is it necessary to sit in the blind for long hours and hope that birds will come in, for if the dog doesn't start them in right away, they aren't coming at all.

If it is so superior, why isn't it more widely practiced? Well, the conditions have to be just right. It can only be done on large, undisturbed lakes. On such a body of water, ducks and geese do raft up far from shore through most of the day, and they are relaxed enough to pay attention to a tolling dog. It will not work on small ponds, nor on the moving waters of our rivers, where birds don't raft. It is not practical even on large lakes where there are a lot of boats or many hunters shooting frequently at decoying or passing waterfowl, for the noise makes the birds too nervous to toll. Thus, tolling has never caught on in this country, and never will. We lack the proper conditions in most of our waterfowling areas.

Therein lies a problem for the dog named for this particular type of work: Few realize that the dog is also a good retriever for normal waterfowling, that he does a nice job as an upland flusher, and that he is an outstanding family pet as well. The name gets in the dog's way and keeps him from realizing the popularity his merits deserve.

The breed is in many ways a smaller version of the very popular Golden Retriever, having a similar appearance and many similar personality traits, so there are surely thousands of potential Toller homes in America today. In fact, the Golden is another Scottish breed, developed in Scotland itself. One can only wonder whether it would have achieved its current popularity had it been named the "Scottish Flushing, Fetching, and Obedience Trial Winning Retriever."

SECTION III:

ACQUIRING YOUR HUNTING RETRIEVER

Since you are still turning these pages, it is reasonable to assume that you are wild to have your very own hunting retriever. Or, that one would really be nice, if only . . . (fill in the blank). Or, that you have been thinking about it for some time and just need a little more information. Or, that, well, you haven't totally ruled out the idea, but this may not be the proper time. Or . . . or . . . or . . .

Clearly, the first step in the acquisition process is deciding whether you should indeed have a hunting retriever. Chapter 12 addresses that decision, and not in the usual everyone-should-have-one manner. Many avid wildfowl hunters are better off without retrievers, even though that means wading or rowing after downed birds. Some maniacal retrieverites seldom fire a shot at wild game, preferring to limit their recreation to field trials and hunting tests. Other maniacal retrieverites hunt several times each week during the season but disdain field trials and hunting tests as too artificial. There is no demographic "map" that fits all people who should own retrievers.

Determining whether you should buy a dog is somewhat like determining whether you should have children. Both depend greatly on your subconscious feelings, and only slightly on your circumstances. I know one young couple that seem ideally suited for parenthood—well-matched, warm, friendly, outgoing, educated, comfortably fixed with an even brighter future—and yet they have decided against children. Unquestionably, they made a good decision *for them*. I know another couple that waited almost too long before having the one and only child they ever wanted. They had to be "sure" they could afford a baby. When their circumstances felt right, they flipped the switch and had a daughter who is now the center of their world. Another good decision. My wife and I had six children in eight years, early in our marriage. We struggled in all the ways middle class parents of large families struggle: financially, emotionally, physically, socially. The punch line of an old joke that went "Yeah, there're all mine and it ain't no picnic," came to mind many times through the years. Still, for us, it was a good decision—or series of them.

This book won't help you decide whether to have children, but it will give you a simple test that will determine whether you should have a retriever.

If your answer is "Yes"—and I make no effort to persuade you in that direction, believe me—I offer you practical recommendations in Chapters 13 and 14 that can help you locate the ideal hunting retriever for your situation. In Chapter 13, I tell you (and you will probably not listen) why a trained dog makes more sense than a puppy as your first retriever. In Chapter 14, I tell you how to maximize the probability that a puppy will work out for you, if you do indeed insist on starting with one.

Then, in Chapter 15 I tell you how to prepare for your dog's arrival. You need to decide where he will live, and if that decision forces you to do some construction work (like a concrete and chain-link "run" in the backyard), you should complete that before the dog arrives.

53

12

SHOULD YOU OR SHOULDN'T YOU?

Okay, you would rather hunt waterfowl than hit golf balls, heave bowling balls, pitch bocci, or ride around in a hot air balloon. Maybe you're such a fanatic that your spouse dares not inquire where he/she stands relative to your passion for ducks and geese. On top of that, perhaps you stomp around in the uplands, too, for pheasant, grouse, prairie chickens, and quail.

You are a conservationist at heart. You count the number of crippled birds that get away each year, and the total bothers you. Something inside has been nagging you to buy a retriever so those birds will not get away next year.

The persuasiveness of the "logic" supporting retrievers rivals that for the breech-loading shotgun. Even a less-than-mediocre retriever will recover downed birds that would escape the unaided hunter—just as the lowest form of breech-loader will down more birds than will the finest of muzzle-loaders.

Ergo, if you shoot a breech-loader, you should have a retriever, right? Not necessarily. The careless hunter who damages a shotgun beyond repair can toss it in the trash, buy another, and abuse the new one if he can afford frequent replacements. A dog suffers physically and/or mentally when not properly cared for, trained, and handled.

Some people—including many very nice folks—should never own dogs. Maybe they don't like them. Maybe they just don't understand them. Regardless of the reason, they frustrate themselves and their dogs with misconceived and inconsistent training.

Even a person who has outstanding rapport with dogs can pass through circumstances that dictate "no dog," at least temporarily. Too much traveling on business. Financial reverses. Long-term illness. Family priorities.

I went through a seven-year period myself when a dog was out of the question.

I receive frequent telephone calls from people thinking about buying retrievers. The "correct" answer in each individual case comes more from my admittedly foggy insight into human nature than my clearer understanding of the place of retrievers in our hunting world.

The caller reveals internal conflict with every word. Something presses him to buy a dog. It may be a friend with an outstanding worker. It may be a friend with a really lousy one: a retriever with which the caller has tired of sharing a blind. It may be a newly found interest in waterfowling and a vague realization of a retriever's value as a conservationist. It may be loneliness, or a recent business failure from which the caller is seeking escape through a warm affectionate, all-forgiving puppy. Whatever the motive, the caller always has an itch that he feels a retriever would scratch.

However, he also has serious doubts. Always. If not, why the call? Perhaps the spouse dislikes dogs. Perhaps the caller must travel a lot and worries that he won't be able to properly care for the animal. Perhaps retriever training looms as black magic in the caller's mind, something which he feels he could never bring off. Perhaps he has always harbored a secret fear of dogs (which is more common than you may think). Perhaps a lot of things, but there is no question that the caller is struggling through a dilemma.

For some reason that psychologists may or may not have classified and named, the caller doesn't want to discuss the sources of his conflict. Instead, he wants to talk about retrievers. Are they friendly? Are they difficult to train? Are they destructive around the house? Do they smell bad? How much do they eat? And on and on.

Sometimes I suspect such a caller wants me to talk him into buying a dog or pup so that he will feel less personally responsible if things don't work out. I used to fall

(Adapted from "Should I Get a Retriever?" *Wildfowl*, October/November, 1985.)

for that, but no more. Instead, I probe until I understand what is *really* motivating the question, after which I simply clarify the options within the caller's frame of reference as best I can and lob the ball back onto his side of the net.

For example, I once received several calls over a period of weeks from a prominent local professional man; a man of stature and influence. Each time he wanted to talk about Golden Retrievers, giving every indication that he would like for me (a known Golden nut) to urge him to rush out and buy one. I didn't. Instead, I drew him out, although it took several calls before he finally opened up:

"Do you hunt?"

"Yes."

"Ever with a dog?"

"No."

"Why start now?"

"Well, my two daughters are twelve and thirteen, and I thought it would be nice if we trained the dog together as a family. They could even show it in obedience and dog shows."

"Have the girls ever had a dog?"

"No."

"Do either of them really want one now?"

"Well, I think so. When I talk to them about it, they seem enthusiastic."

Even with my foggy insight into human nature, I could see that this man, who was accustomed to running his world with a strong hand, realized that his daughters were slipping away. They were—and should have been—discovering boys and all the wonders that have so long allowed one generation to follow another. This frightened Dad. Subconsciously, he felt that he might decoy them away from the opposite sex with a family interest in dog training. Yet, he also knew subconsciously that this wouldn't work, nor would anything else. As far as I know, he didn't buy a dog—which was a good decision for him.

He wasn't unique. Actually, most such callers *shouldn't* buy a dog. Those who should have a retriever don't have to ask anyone. They know. They have no internal conflicts, and they don't care a cup of puppy kibble what I, or anyone else, thinks about their decision.

Who then should have a retriever? That is the easiest question on earth to answer: *The person who simply cannot live without one,* that's who! Let me restate that: The guy or gal who *must* have a retriever *should* have a retriever.

Take me for example. I grew up with dogs. My earliest memories involve a Chow/Shepherd cross named Tuffy. To prevent me from riding my tricycle into the street, he would grab one of the back wheels and hang on, no matter how furiously I kicked at him. Then, there was Scrappy, a Boston Terrier that slept at the foot of my bed and mirrored my changing childhood moods. When I was sick, Scrappy was sicker. When I was well,

he demanded my constant attention. Through high school I had Smokey, a blue Chow that allowed me the space a teenager needs to mature, but he was always there to romp and play when I needed to revert to childhood. Since Smokey, most of my dogs have been hunting dogs: Goldens, Labs, Chesapeakes, Pointers, Setters, Weimaraners, Shorthairs, and Springers.

There was a seven-year period when I couldn't have dogs. We had six small children, one of them severely retarded. That was absolutely all my wife, Theresa, could handle. Even one of my wildly enthusiastic dogs around the place would have pushed her over the brink. I didn't ask. I knew. During that period I tried other recreations. Golf in the summer. Back to graduate school the rest of the year. Nothing took the place of dogs. Breaking 90 meant little. Ditto for picking up one master's degree and parts of two others.

After the worst was over, my wife suggested I get another dog, assuring me she could handle it. The kids were bigger, and our little retarded son had died. I hadn't even mentioned dogs for several years, but she knew how I felt. Elated, I said I wanted a Labrador, but the family voted 6 to 1 for a Golden. I didn't care, just so long as it was a retriever. I was fully alive again—and have been ever since.

The point is: If you *must* have a retriever to feel fully alive, get one. If not, there are a couple of other options.

The better option is to hunt with someone who has a good retriever. With well over 100,000 registered every year, there are a lot of them out there. Perhaps the best way to become acquainted with a hunter who owns a well-trained retriever is to join the local retriever club in your area. Go out to the lease (most clubs have land and water leased for training) and volunteer to do some of the grunt work associated with training, like throwing birds, and planting the birds for blind retrieves. Since finding volunteers to do these chores is a major problem for retriever trainers, the entire membership will quickly see you as a thoroughly charming sort; the most popular member in the club, a guy anyone would love to hunt with. Retriever folks treat good help like royalty. "Would you like to hunt in my blind this fall?" "No, you take the shot. I'm here mostly for the dog work." And so on.

Another option is a "proper" boat; one that is safe on the waters you hunt. You will fail to pick up some birds that a good retriever would bring in, like those that slip into heavy weeds and those that dive and stay down, but with a boat you will recover most of the birds you knock down.

I recommend one or the other of these options to anyone who lacks a strong personal need for a dog. That may seem like a strange recommendation coming from a retriever fanatic like me; however, I have my reasons.

Retrievers are living, sensitive animals that require daily care and attention. I have seen dogs go stir-crazy

If you must *have a retriever to feel fully alive* . . .

You're a conservationist at heart, like Bill Wheeler here who is about to receive a pintail drake from Sonny.

from neglect—especially dogs that were left alone in a small pen in the backyard for unrelieved months during the off-season. The owner of such a psycho dog did all the "right things": fed, watered, and cleaned up after the animal, and so felt that the problem must derive from faulty breeding. Not so. The dog needed companionship, and didn't get it.

The person who lacks a strong need for the companionship of a dog—year-round—will neglect his retriever, if he buys one. Not at first, of course, for the newness of it all and the fact that puppies are so cute will rouse him from his chair in front of the TV for awhile. However, gradually the dog will command less and less of his attention. If the dog lives in the house, he will get attention from some family member, but if the animal is kept in a run outside, his fate is grim indeed.

A glass fiber or aluminum boat would better fit this person's backyard. It won't suffer physical or mental damage from neglect. It won't require food, water, and clean-up work. It won't chew prized possessions.

On the other hand, it won't wag all over when the boss approaches. It won't rub a wet nose on a person's hand after dropping a duck in it. It won't nuzzle a guy's hand in the duck blind until he finds himself unconsciously scratching a canine chin. It won't take that long leap into the icy water for duck after duck on the worst days. It won't sneak a bite of the boss's sandwich, and then look up sheepishly. There are a lot of things the best boat on earth won't do that every dog lover needs done.

If you are such a person, if your life lacks a major component when you don't own a dog, and if you are now considering a retriever, you don't need my advice on whether to get one or not. You would buy one whether I recommended it to you or not. Good for you!

While you don't need my advice before you decide to buy a retriever, I may still be of some small service to you. I can loan you some of my well-tested rationalizations for buying a retriever (or *another* retriever). These rationalizations will allow you to pass yourself off as normal among those who do not share your love for dogs, and who therefore expect you to explain your actions in terms foreign to your true feelings. You and I know that we buy these brutes because we cannot *not* buy them, but most people you and I interact with daily expect a more practical explanation. Here are my best ones. Feel free to use them as is, or to embellish them to better fit your particular needs.

First off, a retriever is a wonderful conservationist. He will pick up birds you would never recover without him. We all know that. We also know that we can in no way cost-justify a dog's initial cost plus year-round maintenance costs based on the total tonnage of increased meat the animal recovers—at least not when applying any rational dollar value to this meat. Nevertheless, to the non-dog-lover, whether a hunter or not, this conservation argument is compelling, even noble-sounding.

Then, there is the family togetherness ploy. "Look, Honey, I'll spend a lot more time with the kids if they are out there throwing birds for me every evening. Besides, it'll get them out from under your feet a couple of hours a day." What hassled house frau could resist that one?

Or, there's the watchdog gambit. "Gee, there's so much crime anymore. I would feel better at the office knowing we have a watchdog at home." Even the anti-hunter will buy into that one, and probably won't realize that most retrievers are too friendly for sentry duty.

There are others: the kids-need-a-dog scheme; the everyone-on-the-block-has-one smokescreen; the profit-from-puppies pipe-dream.

For the more advanced—those rationalizing their second, third, or fourth retriever—I can only say you have to be creative, maybe even a little lucky. For example, I had wanted a Chesapeake for many years, but always had more Goldens and Labs than could be justified by my meager shooting skill. In 1985 my desire for a Chessy became overpowering. However, I knew that even a great lady like my wife would have to be finessed a tad before she would accept still another dog. I also knew that my first swing of the bat would have to be successful; one strike and I would be out, for she would know what I was up to. While I pondered different strategems, the retriever gods smiled on me. Steve Smith called to ask whether I would do a retriever column for *Wildfowl* magazine. That question served up the "fat pitch" I needed. Hanging up, I shared the good news with my unsuspecting spouse, and while she was quietly enjoying it, I slipped in, "A lot of my readers have Chesapeakes. Maybe I should get one. What do you think?"

CRAAACK! Home-run over the center field fence! Beaver, now 90 pounds of brawn, joined the family as a tiny puppy within a week. Like I said, you have to be creative, and a bit lucky.

13

BUYING A TRAINED DOG MAKES SENSE

Still with me? Then, I'll assume you have decided that you can no longer live without a retriever. While you may or may not have had other dogs of other breeds in the past, this will be your first retriever. In this chapter, I will give you some advice relative to how to go about getting the retriever that will best suit your current needs. Most of you will ignore it and buy a seven-week-old puppy—which is, I must admit, what I did when I bought my first retriever—but you should at least read what I have to say here.

By the time he prepares to buy his first retriever, the average American wildfowler carries in his heart a severe case of culture-block against using common sense in the acquisition process.

From childhood he was reared in our sentimental American puppy-pet culture. Every child should grow up with a dog. Every dog starts out as a puppy. Rin-Tin-Tin did. Lassie did. Ditto for every functionless family pet, purebred or mutt, that has ever charmed Mom, Dad, and all the kids. Therefore, when he realizes a need for a working retriever, our hero instinctively feels it would be a sacrilege against the memory of Scrappy, Fifi, or Spike to consider anything but a just-weaned puppy.

Too bad some of the old market hunters aren't around to advise him about that first retriever. To them a dog was a matter of economic survival as well as companionship, so they took a more practical approach.

Today the most practical dog owners, those who could most easily identify with the market hunters' attitudes, share their lives and their work with herding breed animals: Border Collies, Kelpies, Australian Shepherds, and the dozens of other breeds that handle livestock for a living. The common sense of these people derives from the happy fact that their dogs both contribute to their work-

a-day employment and constitute their major form of recreation.

Cattle rancher, L.R. Alexander of Marshfield, Missouri, used to pay three or four mounted hands for routine stock handling. Expensive. Several years ago he decided to economize with a Border Collie. Now, he works his stock with no assistants other than his dogs. This saves him thousands of dollars every year and gives him a lot of enjoyment, too. L.R. loves to work with his dogs so much that they are as much hobby as business.

Sheep rancher, Ric Pinney, who operates near Seattle, Washington, saves a lot of money every year by using his Australian Shepherds. Speaking of their recreational value, he said, "These dogs are my fishing pole. When I am working with them, I have a fishing frame of mind in a golf course environment."

Like the old market hunters, these herding breed owners use their dogs every day. They are close friends with their stock dogs, again like the market hunters. And they choose dogs like the old market hunters did. They have to, as a matter of economic necessity.

Unlike L.R. Alexander, Ric Pinney, and the old market hunters, today's wildfowler cannot realistically claim any economic motivation for maintaining a dog. Perhaps that is why he seldom applies his common sense, seldom even identifies all his options, much less evaluates them. To make this point more clear, for the moment, let's pretend that a retriever would make or save the hunter several thousand a year, and see what the retriever acquisition process looks like from that point of view.

First off, if a retriever affected the profit and loss statement, no ducker could afford to be without one. He would have to learn to love them. As a matter of fact, he would demand a good one—a fully-trained, working animal, not just a pup that "might turn out in a year or so." The only time he could rationally buy a pup would be after he already had a grown dog that got the job done.

(Adapted from "Common Sense Retriever Buying," *Wildfowl,* February/March, 1988.)

The pup would be a "redshirt" working his way into the starting line-up. And the pup would have to show continuous progress on the practice field to remain "on scholarship."

That's the way practical herding breed folks look at things. L.R. Alexander says, "It makes no sense to get sentimental over every dog you try out, but once you get one that really carries its weight around the place, it's okay to get as sentimental as you like. You won't ruin a good working dog by making a pal out of him." Notice he said "dog" throughout, not "puppy."

Looking at it that way does give a broadened perception of the possibilities in the retriever buying process, especially for a "first" retriever. The fully-trained dog makes sense for a mixture of economic and non-economic reasons.

First, there is little or no gamble. The hunter who pulls out his checkbook only after getting acquainted with a trained retriever and seeing him perform knows exactly what he is buying. He knows that he has rapport with the animal. He knows that the dog can do what he needs done. Anything else is a gamble. A pup is a big gamble. A "started" dog is a great or small gamble, depending on what "started" means in the particular seller's vernacular. An untrained adult dog is normally a bad gamble.

And money is only the ante in these games of chance. The real stakes are the months and years of the buyer's life that will pass before he knows whether the pup can cut it. Money is a replenishable resource; time is not. The year or two a wildfowler wastes on a pup that flunks the course represents a sizeable piece of his life that is gone, unrecoverable, spent. Trouble is, most of us go through life thinking we have more time than money, so we pinch pennies while we throw away years on one long-shot after another.

Of course, even the ante can add up to significant coinage if a person goes through several pups before one of them works out. That is not unusual. Not every pup from even the finest breeding has the right instincts. Further, a beginner can easily ruin a good prospect with poorly conceived training. By the time an unlucky novice ruins enough dogs to learn how to train one properly—and then acquires a decent pup to work with—he could be out the price of a new car (or a fully-trained retriever) and still have nothing.

Another advantage of the fully-trained retriever is that the seller will certainly spend enough time with the buyer to make sure the latter knows how to handle the animal, knows what verbal and non-verbal cues must be used to bring out its best qualities. He will even go through the training procedures so the buyer will be able to do routine maintenance on his own. Even the most perfectly trained dog needs a little brush-up periodically, so it is important that the new owner understand how his fully-trained retriever got that way in the first place.

Such handling and training information will not only help the buyer with this particular dog, it will prepare him for the day when he buys a puppy and starts from scratch. He will have several years of experience working with a trained dog behind him, which will give him better insight into puppy training.

Which brings up another reason for starting with a fully-trained dog: it precludes the discouragement that turns so many new dog owners off, and makes house-pets of so many potentially good retriever pups. Bringing a pup along from scratch will lead even the experienced trainer through some puzzling days. Many beginners simply give up, deciding they were never cut out to train dogs.

The old market hunters would advise you to start with a trained dog.

There is one disadvantage to starting with a fully-trained retriever: INITIAL COST. Such animals change hands for figures that occupy four, and sometimes five spaces on a ledger sheet. Big bucks, indeed. True, this is a bargain for anyone who can afford it. A dog that does multiple marks and blind retrieves on land and in water has passed through a lot of days in someone's training program. He has also succeeded where other dogs have washed out, and the buyer, whether he realizes it or not, pays his share of that sort of overhead, just as he does when he buys a spread of decoys or a duck boat.

Where can the well-heeled ducker find such a virtuous retriever? His best bet is to contact a few professional trainers around the country. (See Appendix II.) If he offers to pay the pro's phone expenses plus a reasonable finder's fee, one of them will locate the dog of his dreams more rapidly than he imagines possible. If the buyer is really clever, he will have a different pro evaluate the dog for thirty days before he completes the purchase. This evaluation won't be cheap, but it makes sense, like having a painting or antique independently appraised before buying it.

Anyone with enough money-smarts to be able to afford the price of a new car for his first retriever will quickly grasp the idea that the fully-trained animal is a bargain in the long run. He will realize that he would probably spend that much (or more!) before he gets the dog he wants, no matter how he starts. It's just a question of one big initial payment for the fully-trained dog, or a steady negative cash flow over a longer period with the other options. And, he understands the value of time. A fully-trained dog is NOW, and certain. A puppy is a year or two off, and MAYBE.

However, the average *paterfamilias* doesn't have such liquid assets lying around idle, nor is he willing to liquidate significant family holdings to go first class on a retriever. True, if he were a rancher buying a Border Collie that would save thousands of bucks per annum, he could develop a cost/benefit analysis that would justify borrowing several thou up-front. However, this is a retriever, which will never turn a dime and which will probably create some minor havoc from time to time within the spouse's hallowed domain. Realistically, anyone who is so hopelessly middleclass (as most of us are) that he routinely coordinates major purchases with his significant-other will never sell the idea of a fully-trained retriever.

However, that doesn't mean the less affluent duck blind habitué should resign himself to dribbling out twice the price of such a dog over the next several years on a long line of puppies that don't make it. The "started dog" is the next best thing to the fully-trained retriever. The up-front money required will be substantially less (several hundred to a few thousand), and the started dog already has some capabilities.

A started dog can be anything from a youngster that hasn't yet learned about double marks to a field trial washout that has started training on blind retrieves. At

The seller of a trained dog will teach you how to handle it even if he has to "play dog" for you.

the very least, he should be young (under two years), love birds, be obedience-trained, steady, deliver to hand, and do solid work on single marks out to 100 yards on land and in water. Anything less simply is not a started dog—and may be a pawn in somebody's rip-off scheme.

I have heard of one mail order entrepreneur who stocks his kennel with whatever sporting dogs he finds in the local pound, and advertises them nationally at bargain prices as "started." When some innocent orders a dog from him, this operator ships whatever he has in that breed at the moment. Naturally, the buyer complains, so the friendly fleecer offers the frustrated fleecee a replacement dog "that you will surely like." Money back instead? No way in hell—just a replacement. Naturally, all shipping costs are paid by the buyer. After several such replacements, the typical buyer wearies of paying round-trip airfare for one worthless mutt after another, so he writes it all off to experience and gives up.

Cute, eh? This person is the exception, of course, for most sellers are honest. However, remember that if you are the *emptor,* (buyer) don't forget to *caveat* (beware). Here, as in the case of the fully-trained dog, the buyer's best friend is a professional trainer with contacts all over the country. For expenses and a negotiated fee he will find a started dog that will meet any reasonable expectations, especially if there is a possibility that said pro may be asked to finish the training.

The pro can tell the buyer whether the dog is worth buying from a performance point of view. However, only the future owner can determine whether he personally can get along amiably with it. (I have known many outstanding retrievers with which I would have had serious personality conflicts.) The smart buyer will spend time with the prospect, and resolutely resist any animal he doesn't warm up to. The right dog for him is the one he can't help but like.

A started dog will retrieve ducks as soon as the season opens. The neophyte whistle-tooter and his new dog will succeed and have fun together the first time they share a blind. That fact alone will give the guy a positive outlook on the future training.

But, what about starting with a pup?

Several years ago, I hankered to burn a little black powder. Instead of plunking down the $100 to $150 that a ready-to-shoot replica Colt cost at the time, I decided to save money by buying a kit for about $60. Before I could go out and actually push lead balls with pungent powder, I had to build my own gun from the bewildering array of tiny pieces in the box I brought home. To fit the parts together I had to file a bit, assemble a bit, experiment a bit, then disassemble completely to file some more. Time after time I did this. Eventually, I overdid the filing and ruined the kit. I bought another. I screwed that one up too. That put me out about the price of a ready-to-shoot gun, and all I had for my money was two boxes

full of worthless parts. Discouraged, I decided that black powder shooting just wasn't my game.

A friend of mine did it the right way. He bought a ready-to-shoot replica .36 1851 Navy and started enjoying the hobby immediately. Then, he bought another gun, this one a .44 Walker replica, and shot both of them. Eventually, after he was really into the sport and had met some folks who could help him if he got into trouble, he bought a kit and built a gun of his own. Of course, his attitude toward the kit was more relaxed than mine because it didn't matter whether he succeeded with the first kit (or the tenth, for that matter) since he had a couple of guns to shoot. He still punches round holes in assorted targets on weekends, while I never got started.

The analogy with retrievers is obvious. And there are any number of others that are equally valid. Lots of people build their own fly rods, but not their first ones. Ditto for decoy whittling, radio-controlled modeling (airplanes, cars, trains), boat building, and home tailoring.

However, most American first-retriever buyers look instinctively for a just-weaned puppy, without analyzing the other options. True, many succeed in spite of the odds against them—mostly those with knowledgeable friends to help them, and those who can get assistance from the puppy's breeder. Years ago when I bred a litter now and then, I always invited local puppy buyers to join my training group. This allowed me to watch my stock develop, and provided me with extra bird-throwers. More important for our present discussion, it gave many novices an opportunity to learn how to train their dogs.

If you have never trained a retriever, and if you insist on starting with a puppy, you will almost certainly fail unless you have guidance from some knowledgeable person. Thus, it makes sense for you to locate the experienced help you will need—a friend, the breeder, a pro—before you fall in love with a particular puppy.

If you don't, you may well join the many people who call me (and others around the country) so often and say something like this:

"I've got this really great retriever. He's two years old now, and I haven't given him any training, but with just a little work, he'd be one of the best in the country. Unbelievable pedigree. Lots of champions and field champions. I don't really have time to train him, and to tell the truth, he's driving my wife crazy. So much energy. Do you know someone who would like to have this dog?"

Sorry. I don't know anyone who would accept such an animal as a gift. In our American puppy-pet culture, the untrained adult dog is the most difficult of all retrievers to place. That is why so many of them end up in the pound, where most are put down and some may be picked up by unscrupulous operators for resale as started dogs.

Think about it: Doesn't that little puppy you are thinking about buying deserve a better end than that?

14

BUT IF YOU MUST HAVE A PUPPY

As I have stressed in the previous chapter, the hunter should select as his *first* retriever a grown dog that is as completely trained as the individual can afford. That makes sense from every point of view. The dog will perform useful work on opening day of the first season, and thereafter for many years. The cost will probably be less than one typically incurs gambling on a series of puppies that fail to make the grade. The buyer will learn how to handle his dog from the seller, and how to do routine maintenance training, all of which will make it easier for him to develop his own pup later.

Yet, no matter how practical the grown dog may be, most first-time retriever buyers prefer to gamble on puppies. They happily toss the dice, disregarding all the ways they can come up snake-eyes. The dog may contract one of the many puppy diseases and die. The puppy may never exhibit the hunting and retrieving instincts that have endeared his breed to hunters for generations. The new owner may make so many mistakes that he ruins a most promising youngster. Worse (and more common), he may never begin the pup's training program, for any of several reasons: The owner's enthusiasm may wane; his marital, familial, or occupational circumstances may suffer the "slings and arrows of outrageous fortune"; a personality conflict may develop between dog and human.

On the other hand, if the puppy buyer throws a seven, an eleven, or if he makes his "point" after a few extra tosses of the dice, he wins more than the grown-dog buyer can ever buy. He wins the deep satisfaction of developing his own working retriever. There's nothing like it.

So, if you are one of those who prefers to take a chance on a puppy, realizing that it may take several pups and as many years from your life before you get what you seek, I understand your attitude. While I am long past my first dog, and therefore not so significantly at risk as most puppy buyers, I must admit that I belong to their club. In spite of frequent disappointments from even the noblest breedings, in spite of the fact that each such disappointment takes a proportionally larger chunk of my remaining life, I will probably maintain my membership as long as I have breath enough to blow a whistle.

There is something special about bringing a pup along from scratch. The author here works with Belvedere's Rhett Butler.

(Adapted from ''Selecting a Retriever Pup,'' *Waterfowler's World,* October/November, 1985; and ''The Right Upland Dog for You,'' *Wind and Shot,* January/February, 1988).

As I mentioned earlier, I once struggled two frustrating years with a Labrador whose pedigree was so royal that I felt unworthy to share her home. Trouble was, her hunting desire came and went, making her much like the little girl with the little curl in the middle of her forehead. Another time I wasted four years (!) on a borderline Golden. She looked like a world-beater in the summer, but in the fall she was offended that I should ask her to jump into that cold water just for a silly duck that, after all, I—not she—had shot.

On the other hand, I have many times had the overwhelming joy of watching a pup develop from birth to finished performer status (partially because of, partially in spite of, my training). Nothing can rival the total understanding you have of a dog you have brought along from its first breath. You know the dog's strengths and weaknesses, which of the latter to correct and which to work around—and how to do both. You know what training steps underlie the dog's performance, which ones to repeat when a problem comes up. Most of all, you have the love and respect of that particular animal as no other human ever will.

Yeah, I like puppies, even though I know they make less and less sense as I grow older. Having had a seeming jillion of them, I can tell you how to minimize your risk—not eliminate it—if you decide to go with a raw puppy. I must admit that I haven't always followed my own advice. Perhaps that is why I'm sure it is good advice.

There are only four considerations: breed, sex, litter, and individual puppy—and they should be taken up in that order.

Among the eight retrievers, breed selection should baffle no one. All eight breeds can do whatever today's waterfowler needs done. The frequently-touted arguments that such-and-such a breed is superior to all others under such-and-such circumstances are wonderful for stimulating lively conversation in the clubhouse or at the Christmas party. However, they are meaningless in the duckblind or in the uplands. Today's hunting conditions and bag limits prevent each breed from demonstrating the particular type of "superiority" for which it was developed. For example, the tireless water- and weather-proof Chesapeake may have served the nineteenth century market hunter better than any other retriever when hundreds of birds lay on the surface of the water requiring constant work all day and into the night; but how can anyone say this superiority carries over to our times, when one is lucky to fill a three-mallard limit? Ditto for the other breeds' forte, whatever it once was.

A litter of pups, like these Rumrunner Goldens bred by the author, are hard to resist.

Breed selection is simple: Pick the one that most appeals to you. All of them can do the job you need a retriever to do, but each breed is unique physically and mentally. One breed will suit you personally better than all the rest. This book contains a profile of each breed, and should help you identify the breed that you would like to have around the place, to train and hunt. Pay attention to your gut reactions to these profiles. Realize that no breed has "good" and/or "bad" traits, but merely a peculiar set of traits that appeal to certain people. The traits you like will displease others. No one breed is superior, except in the eyes of its admirers.

Which sex should you choose? Whichever you want to choose! It matters not a rat's rear as far as effectiveness afield is concerned whether you have a boy puppy or a girl puppy. As proof, let me offer this prediction: whichever sex you choose, you will encounter an "expert" who will bore you for a whole evening explaining why you should have gone with the other sex.

Having selected a breed and a sex, you should next pick a particular litter of puppies. This will challenge anyone who has selected one of the rarer breeds (any except the Labrador, Golden, and Chesapeake) but that should not induce such a person to opt for the more popular breeds. To find a breeder for the seven AKC-recognized breeds, contact the national breed club (addresses for all of them are in Appendix II).

Once you have located a few breeders, visit those in your vicinity and call or write those farther away. The information you should seek is as follows:

1. What breeding goals have they set for themselves? (Field trials, hunting tests, dog shows, obedience trials.)

2. What success have they had to date (titles, etc.)?

3. What breedings do they plan for the near future? Here you need specifics about the accomplishments of the sire, dam, and all four grandparents. Dogs farther back in the pedigree should be disregarded.

4. Do they breed only sires and dams that are free from hereditary hip, eye, and other problems? What kind of health guarantee do they offer puppy buyers?

5. Can they give you references (previous puppy buyers you can contact) especially for repeat breedings?

6. What do they charge for a puppy? Do they require a deposit? How do they determine who gets which pick from the litter?

7. Do they remove dewclaws? (They should.) Give preliminary shots? (They should.)

8. Will the pups be introduced to birds and water before leaving the litter?

With this information from several breeders, you should be able to select a litter or two. Study the pedigrees. If you know nothing of pedigrees in your chosen breed, find someone other than the breeder who can help you with this. When you are satisfied with a particular pedigree, visit the breeder's place (if possible), look at his dogs, even see some of them work. If things there make you comfortable, plunk down a deposit and wait for the puppies to hit the ground.

So much for selecting the litter. While you are waiting to pick your puppy, spend your time getting ready for his arrival at your home. First, decide where he will live (you will find my personal recommendation in the next chapter). Build or buy whatever housing you need. Buy the collars, leads, training dummies, whistles, and other

Sheila Spencer teaches her puppy, Rumrunner's Pirate, to come-in on command.

This is how the author started Duffy in water.

retriever accouterments. Join the local retriever club. Buy books on training. Subscribe to appropriate magazines. In other words, prepare for your puppy's arrival.

If possible, go to the breeder's place to select your puppy. You have probably heard and read about all sorts of tests that are intended to help you pick the "best field prospect" from the litter: Toss a pigeon out and see which pup gets to it first; roll each pup on his back and see how he reacts; toss a tennis ball for each pup to see how strong his retrieving instinct is; leave each pup, walk away, squat down, and clap your hands to see which comes to you most readily; and on and on. My personal recommendation? Do all of these things, then run through any other "fool-proof" test you may have heard of—and then select the puppy that you *just plain like best,* the one with which you feel the strongest rapport, the one that comes across as your kind of dog. The results of the various tests? Forget them. You only went through them to allow yourself an opportunity to interact with each pup.

That is the beauty of a litter. There is no one best pup among them, for the best dog for you will probably not be the best one for me. *Rapport* is the one essential ingredient, and different people establish rapport with different canine personalities.

If you cannot visit the breeder and pick your own puppy, call him and explain the personality type you want. Dependent or independent. Sensitive or hard-headed. Relaxed or energetic. Conscientious breeders spend many hours every day with their litters. They understand each pup's personality, and are more anxious than you are to see you matched up with the right youngster.

Years ago I met an elderly Pointer breeder who had an outstanding local reputation. With very little coaxing I induced him to tell me his secret: He matched each pup with the right buyer on the basis of temperament.

"While the guy is fooling around with the litter," he chuckled, "I take his wife aside and ask her what he is *really* like—sensitive, hard-headed, hot-tempered, patient, what? Wives know, and they tell me. Then, I just help the guy pick out the puppy that suits his temperament. Works almost every time."

I have picked out some of my puppies and relied on the breeder for others. Frankly, I can't tell any difference in the results. While the overall percentage of pups that turned out to be the kind of retrievers I hoped for when I wrote out the check has been depressingly low—I have said all along pups are a gamble—I can't honestly say that the success ratio among my own picks has exceeded that

65

of the various breeders. Of course, I have always explained to them—perhaps in boring detail—the personality type I have been most successful with (hyperactive, sensitive, affectionate, birdy).

How much should you have to pay for a well-bred puppy? Whatever the breeder asks will be a bargain, believe me. Have you ever noticed that the best breeders make their livings some other way. They aren't in it for the money; they want to improve the breed, leave their mark on future generations of dogs and hunters alike. Puppy sales simply will not recover the dollars they spend buying, raising, training, and proving (in trials and tests) their breeding stock, not to mention their equipment costs and health costs. Just as you cannot justify your hunting with the meat you put on the table, so the breeder cannot support his operation with the income from puppies. Why do you think the IRS demonstrates such skepticism when they come across a return that claims dog breeding as a side business?

If your goal is a successful dog purchase—one you will wish you could repeat years from now when the dog dies—you should adopt a realistic attitude toward price. It is, as a mathematician would say, inversely related to risk. The less you spend the greater your risk, starting with the bargain basement puppy with no pedigree quality and going all the way up through the high dollar fully-trained dog. True, you might turn a give-away pup from down the street into a stem-winder of a duck dog. However, if you ever do, please rush out a buy an Irish Sweepstakes ticket, for the gambling gods are surely smiling on you.

Most of us have to make do with more rational choices based on rational evaluations of price and risk. Even so, whatever we pay will be cheap when spread over the dog's entire life, say ten or twelve years. It is your attitude toward the purchase after those years that should concern you now. If you are reasonably satisfied that you will one day wish you could do it all again, go ahead—pull out your checkbook and uncap your pen. If not, keep looking. After all, those years are going to come out of your life.

This litter of Ardunacres kennel Tollers appears ready for anything. (Photo by Arline MacDonald, Ardunacres Kennel.)

15

PROPER HOUSING

Having decided to buy either a fully-trained retriever, a started retriever, or a puppy, you now must plan for his arrival at your palace and grounds. Too often, major decisions about housing are made haphazardly after the animal has been unloaded at the door. The more rational approach is to make these decisions as early as possible so you can implement them before your new retriever's E.T.A.

Sometimes we, especially we men, concentrate on the obvious while overlooking the less apparent (but equally important). Like the time many years ago when our oldest son, then an infant, had to have surgery. Driving home from the hospital the night before the operation, I felt that Johnny's situation was as good as it could be, but my wife Theresa sniffled softly in the darkness.

"Look," I said, "he's in a nice room, has 24-hour care, an outstanding surgeon. Under the circumstances, what more could he want, for crying out loud?"

"He's just a baby," she sobbed, "and there's no one to hug him and talk to him when he wakes up in the middle of the night."

My concern had been for the physical, so I was only half right. Hers extended beyond the physical to the emotional. I must admit that, over the years, Theresa has brought me a long way, but sometimes I still fail to see the whole picture.

We make a similar mistake when we limit our thinking about dog housing to the physical needs of the animal.

I remember years ago living near a family that had a Brittany penned up out back in a 3'x15'x4' enclosed run with dirt floor and a doghouse. This wasn't a family pet, for the wife and kids were not allowed to play with the beast—after all, it was Dad's hunting dog, and anyone knows you can't make a pet of a hunting dog! (How long

will that sadistic nonsense persist in our society?) This poor Brit spent most of his life in "solitary confinement." Too busy for regular year-round training, Dad did hunt the animal a few weekends each fall. During the rest of the year he fed the Brittany every evening, watered him morning and evening, and cleaned up the pen every other day. That was it. No work, no play, no petting, no nothing.

The animal always appeared physically strong and healthy, but his mind went downhill over the years of almost total isolation. Few things are as sad a watching a "well-cared for" dog go through the stages of emotional starvation: from soft-eyed whining to hard-staring viciousness.

Actually, that Brit's physical environment wasn't too inferior to what my own dogs were living in at the time. True, my runs were larger and on concrete. True also, I cleaned mine twice a day. Nevertheless, my neighbor's setup was not unreasonable.

The big difference which allowed my dogs to thrive in both body and spirit, was companionship. Not only human, but also canine. I worked my dogs in the field several times each week, did the usual amount of obedience training in the yard, and let my kids play with them as long as they followed certain rules, like not throwing sticks and not playing tug-of-war. I must admit that through the really cold spells during the winter, I probably didn't give my dogs any more personal attention than my neighbor did his poor Brit. However, I had two dogs in adjacent runs, so they were able to keep each other company when I was a bit neglectful.

If you are thinking about ways to house your dog(s), your *first* concern—before any consideration of run size, doghouse construction, sanitation, or pest control—should be companionship. Human companionship. Perhaps also canine companionship.

(Adapted from "Canine Castle Considerations," *Wing and Shot,* March/April, 1988.)

Frankly I feel that the one-dog owner should keep his animal in the house, not out in the backyard. Most yapping, half-mad dogs in the fenced yards of urban and suburban America are solitary pets that are never allowed in the house—stir-crazy dogs unable to compete with TV, little league, clubs, and parties for their owners' attention. The house dog, on the other hand, will find ways to get the attention he needs from someone in the family; more often than not, every member will fool with him quite a bit, without even realizing it.

If sharing the family domicile with one dog is an impossibility, there are two rational choices: Forego buying a dog, or buy two. I have little confidence in the oft-mentioned third choice, namely putting one dog out back with a promise to pay it daily court. Sure, the ten-year husband who still faithfully performs whatever galantries he pledged during his premarital madness might succeed in this. However, most people who must struggle through life with a more normal dose of human nature will not long persist.

Two dogs constitute my personal lower limit for any thought of outdoor housing. Two dogs can keep each other company during those periods when the weather, work, or the wayward winds of parental responsibility prevent papa and/or mama from doing the right thing by the family bird dogs. There are other advantages. Two dogs can ''spell'' each other during a day's upland hunt, thereby allowing papa/mama fresh ''wheels'' for the excellent hunting just before sunset. Further, since so much of one's training time is spent getting to and from the grounds, it takes little longer per session to train two dogs than it does just one. The only thing that absolutely doubles with the second dog is the feed bill. Even so, maintaining two dogs makes substantial sense for the uplander who likes to hunt with a dog.

Okay, you have two dogs and want to quarter them properly in your backyard. What constitutes ''properly''?

First, let's eliminate all thought of just allowing young ''Blink'' and ''Bolt'' to run loose in the fenced backyard. They will inflict destruction beyond your wildest imaginings. Lawn, flowers, shrubs, bird bath, patio furniture, hoses, water outlets, decorative fences, screens, barbeque grill, playground equipment, kid's toys—nothing is sacred. Besides, those two conscienceless adventurers will sometimes escape your perimeter to spread discord throughout the neighborhood, especially when you are away at work.

Please, do yourself, your family, and your neighbors a kindness: Put each dog in an escape-proof, separate (but adjoining) kennel run. The ideal geometry for each run is about 20 feet long by 4 feet wide by 6- to 7-feet high (depending on your own height). Those dimensions give Blink and Bolt plenty of running room, while making it easy for you to completely enclose each run. The back, side, and top should be chain-link, or some other study

Every dog needs human companionship—plenty of it. A little ''lap time'' does wonders for the outside dog.

fencing material. The front should be a large matching gate.

The base should be some material that is easy to keep clean. While concrete is best for most of us ordinary hunter-types, many who also show their dogs in conformation feel that concrete splays canine feet, so they opt for coarse gravel and rock. This has more ''give'' as a dog moves across it, but is much harder to clean up. Some people build their runs without any base, leaving just bare ground underneath. That is impossible to clean—really. Besides, it allows the dog to dig out unless Hurculean efforts are made to prevent it (like burying the fence below the probable digging depth or edging the run in concrete, which will eventually make a water hole of it.)

As I said, concrete is best for most of us: permanent, easy to clean, escape-proof, and frankly I have not had any problem with splayed feet on it, either. Whatever material you choose, make sure to install it with sufficient slope to allow good drainage away from the doghouses.

In summary, then, the ideal kennel run should be approximately 20 feet long, 4 feet wide, and 6- to 7-feet high. It should be completely enclosed with chain-link or some similarly stout material, and it should be on a concrete base that is sloped for good drainage away from the doghouses.

Fine, you ask, but what constitutes a ''proper'' doghouse?

68

Before you start design and construction, you should understand the functions of the doghouse. It is there to keep the dog warm and dry during those periods when Mother Nature has other ideas. The dry part is relatively easy: Just make sure the house is watertight and has a doorway that is either covered or pointed with the prevailing wind. It should also be elevated 4- to 6-inches off the ground to protect its resident from flooding.

Unlike the human dwelling, the doghouse does not provide warmth in and of itself. The dog does that, generating body heat just like all other land mammals, including the humanoid variety. All the doghouse does is assist him to retain as much of his own heat as possible. Thus, the ideal doghouse offers draft-free insulation and is as small as is comfortable for the particular dog. Excessive size only creates more space to be heated. Further, since heat rises, tall houses are an abomination. The ideal one should be so short that the dog can just barely walk inside without crouching. It should be only big enough in circumference to allow the dog to curl up without lying directly in front of the entrance. Since heat is transferred to and from the base concrete so readily, the doghouse elevation of 4- to 6-inches is for warmth as well as for protection against flooding.

While the canine dwelling should be draft-free, it should not be air-tight, for the dog must breathe while he snuggles within. Some air should come in through the entrance, even if it is partially covered against wind and water.

Those are the basic doghouse requirements: low-profiled, reasonably small, waterproof, elevated, draft-free but not air-tight, providing good insulation to allow the dog to retain his own body heat. There are more ways of satisfying those requirements than I could list in an entire volume. Some use stout wooden barrels on posts. Others build artistically satisfying houses from one kind of material or another (glass fibre, brick, fancy woods), with all the attractive flair one expects in a high-dollar human domicile. Personally, I prefer simple double-built half-inch plywood or wafer-board construction standing on 4- to 6-inch legs. I separate the inner from the outer walls (and floors) with 1- by 2-inch boards, which leaves an insulating space all around the dog. I build a similar double-built top and make it removable (for ease of cleaning as well as accessibility to a sinning canine in hiding). The roof slope should suit the amount of snow received in the area: steeply sloping roofs for areas of heavy snow accumulations, flat for areas of little snow. A flat roof offers the inhabitant a nice place to sun himself during moderate weather. I had one Golden Retriever that would lie on his rooftop even during a snowstorm.

Floor plans for the ideal doghouse? Naw. I feel that if you understand the functions of the structure, you will be able to design and build one that will not only perform those functions but will also satisfy your personal tastes better than anything I might suggest.

So much for protection from rain and cold. Proper canine quarters must also prevent discomfort and stroke in summer heat. For this, position is more important than construction. You can't build a cool run or doghouse (unless you can afford air-conditioning), but you can locate it in a shady place where there is normally a pleasant breeze.

A large area of shade is absolutely necessary to your dogs' survival in the summer, especially on runs with concrete or other artificial bases. A small, moving patch of shade under a piece of tarpaulin will not suffice. Concrete heats up under the direct rays of the sun, and the heat transfers rapidly from one end to the other. The entire run, or at least a substantial percentage of it, should be shaded if it is to be a bearable surface on which a dog can lie. I have several times seen someone's dog crawl into his doghouse to escape the ground heat in a run with a small piece of material on top for shade. It wasn't all that cool in the doghouse, but when you can fry hamburgers on the concrete, what's a dog to do?

A mature tree is the best possible source of shade, better than anything that can be constructed, for a tree allows normal airflow. A large canvas, wooden, or metal cover over the run is better than nothing, but just barely, as I learned quite by accident a few years ago. My current runs are beneath a huge maple, so they are well shaded and cool. For reasons I can't remember, I one summer tossed a 12-foot john-boat on top of one of them. For several days after that I noticed that that particular run was much warmer than the others when I went in to clean it up. I had forgotten about the boat, so it took me a while to figure out what the problem was. When I did, I removed the boat, and the temperature in that run returned to normal.

If you must construct shade, build it a couple of feet above the top of the run, to allow better air movement. Make sure that the shade covers most of the run most of the time. After you have it properly built, plant a tree—a fast-growing, leafy tree—to take the place of your homemade shade someday.

Sanitation is the next important issue, and that is up to you—on a day-in, day-out basis. Your dogs should not live in filth, either their own or that of birds. It is your job to pick up your dogs' droppings at least once, and better, twice a day. After the pickup chore, you should use a power nozzle to hose the run down until it is immaculate.

Pests and parasite control is an unending battle in which your veterinarian is your best ally. Consult him/her for information about local problems and treatments.

Where is the ideal location for your kennel runs? While many disagree with me, I feel they should be as close to the back door as possible. Mine are no more than four feet from the back of my house, the nearest gate about ten feet from my back door. Located there, they facilitate all my dog-maintenance chores. Feeding is easy. Loading up for training or hunting is easy. Quieting a barking dog is easy. Socializing is easy. I have never understood those who place their kennels 100 yards or more from the house. To me that is just 100 yards of unnecessary walking at least a couple of times a day—sometimes in driving rain, sometimes through drifted snow, sometimes in a stabbing north wind.

What about doubling up two or more dogs in a single run? Personally, I am against it. Too many bad things can happen: fights, accidental injuries, filthy habit development, and so on. I prefer keeping Blink in one run and Bolt in a separate, but adjacent one. The left-side fence of one run should be the right-side fence of the other. That way, they can play and commune with one another, perhaps even swap tall tales in canine-ese: ''You wouldn't believe what old hammerhead did when he was training me today; listen, this is a good one . . .'' However, they cannot get at each other, each other's houses, each other's food, or (frankly) each other's stools.

A large kennel with many adjacent runs resembles an urban neighborhood. The dogs provide companionship to one another and share the services provided by the ''mayor'' and his staff. While most of those services address the dogs' physical well-being, that alone is not enough. The mayor should also socialize his constituents with frequent training sessions and a reasonable amount of individual camaraderie.

While judging a NAHRA hunting test in 1987, I spent a few days at Clarke and Glenda Campbell's Country Kennels near Westgate, Iowa. There I saw an outstanding example of individual socialization at a professional kennel. The resident corps of bird dogs and retrievers are kept outside in a set of adjacent runs such as those I have been discussing here. However, Clarke and Glenda bring a different dog into the house early each evening for a night of housepet status and image-building. They keep the dog with them until morning. Drathaars, Chesapeakes, Labradors, puppies, youngsters, old-timers—they follow a regular rotation. Each dog gets his/her individual turn at being the featured house guest. The salutary effects of this nightly routine shows in the rapport Clarke and Glenda have with these dogs—in training, too, I might add.

Rapport should not be overlooked when you decide how you will house your retriever(s). He needs physical comfort, true. Canine companionship is nice, true. However, rapport with you is what makes Blink and Bolt good team players when you go chasing birds together.

Outdoor kenneling requires at least two dogs—for companionship.

A good kennel run consists of double-built doghouses, concrete base, chainlink sides and top, near the house, and under a shade tree.

SECTION IV:

THE HUNTING RETRIEVER OWNER'S WORLD

"Not by bread alone does man live . . ." And not by hunting alone does the retrieverite live.

Look at it realistically. Hunting contributes significantly to one's mental health. Spiritual cleansing awaits any mortal who arises early, dresses warmly, totes excessive impedimenta, artistically spreads decoys according to family traditions, huddles with a retriever in a wet and miserable blind, blows his call with the narcissism of an 'arteeest,' shoots poorly enough to spend hours limiting out, and comes home after dark to face the unfaceable chores of unloading his pickup, feeding his dog, cleaning his birds, swabbing the bores of his shotgun, and—at last, at last—cleaning and feeding his weary body. Ditto for upland game hunting, with miles of walking through brambles and briars, uphill and down, slogging in mud, wading through deep snow, wearily relaxing just before the dog puts a bird in the air, missing easy shots, missing average shots, occasionally hitting a shot beyond human capability (especially in retrospect), arriving home with a dog full of burrs, a game bag half-full of birds, a gun with major water in its innards, and a weary, hungry body.

The trouble is, we can only hunt in the fall, leaving us a non-hunting period which lasts about 80 percent of the year. Those who really enjoy working with retrievers have developed any number of ways to include their dogs in their off-season activities: field trials, working certificate tests, hunting retriever tests. They have also formed any number of organizations of retriever owners intended to conduct these activities: national breed clubs, retriever field trial and hunting test clubs, obedience training clubs, kennel clubs. As a new retriever owner, you need to know about these activities and these organizations.

This section of the book explains them. Appendix II gives you names and addresses to contact when you want more information, or want to participate. Look over these activities and organizations. They will offer you opportunities to enjoy your retriever during the long off-season. I sincerely encourage you to participate in those activities that appeal to you and join the appropriate organizations.

16

FIELD ACTIVITIES FOR RETRIEVERITES

Retrieverites who hanker for field work "ain't never had it so good." Time was when the choices were like those for the color on a Model T: whatever you want as long as you want AKC-licensed field trials. No more. Innovations in non-competitive testing formats of one kind or another have changed all that. First, several of the national breed clubs initiated various "working certificate" tests, in which a person can prove the worth of his retriever(s) in the field by passing certain prescribed tests. More recently the "hunting retriever movement" has introduced three different types of non-competitive tests, in which the dogs achieve field titles by successfully completing a set of tests prescribed in written standards.

Why do we need so many different field activities for retrievers? Or, what is wrong with AKC-licensed field trials?

AKC-LICENSED FIELD TRIALS

What is wrong with field trials? Absolutely nothing, if you can afford them. Field trials have made today's talented retrievers possible, and anyone who claims that a field trial dog isn't a good hunter either has never hunted with one or has an aversion to truth. The trouble is, only about ten percent of today's retriever owners can afford serious field trial competition.

Back in the early 1900s, the American economic aristocracy brought the Labrador Retriever to this country from England, where they had seen the dogs work while vacationing and hunting there. Many of these wealthy Americans also "imported" some of the better English and Scottish trainers and employed them as full-time managers of newly established but extensive breeding and training kennels. Luxury was the norm. These transplanted British trainers sometimes transported Labradors to the early field trials in one of the boss's spare Duesenbergs or Rolls-Royces—and not in the trunk, either, but seated on the passenger seat. First class all the way.

These affluent Lab folks designed and implemented AKC-licensed field trials specifically for Labradors that had the benefit of full-time professional training on the finest of training grounds. Previously, average American waterfowlers had conducted less formal water trials for our native retriever, the Chesapeake Bay. However, the new (highly promoted) Lab trials introduced extensive land work and eased up on water work, making the Chessy look like a bib-overalled farmer racing his tractor at Indianapolis.

After World War II, because of our blossoming economy, licensed field trials attracted a larger and larger following as more people moved up the financial ladder. This changed trials, but didn't make them any cheaper. Today, most professional trainers are independent businessmen rather than employees of the wealthy. Nevertheless, most of the dogs that win are Labradors that are trained full-time by a pro on excellent training grounds. Only those doctors, lawyers, and Indian chiefs who can pay a pro about $400 per month per dog year-round for the dog's entire active life can afford to play. The broad American middle-middle class, the folks who own most of this country's retrievers today, lack the "ante" to get into the game—not to mention the "table stakes" to back a strong hand.

Even so, field trials have been responsible for development of the outstanding lines of retrievers extant today in the various breeds. The talented pros who dominate trials have improved the breeds, especially the Labrador, beyond the wildest dreams of those who imported the first ones.

(Adapted from "Field Activities for Retrieverites," *Breed and Show,* February, 1985.)

There are four "stakes" in a field trial. Each stake is a separate and independent competition among the entered dogs. Four "placements" (first through fourth) are awarded in each stake. If a non-placing dog completes all tests satisfactorily, he receives a Judge's Award of Merit (JAM). Each of the four stakes has different requirements for entry. The "Derby" stake is limited to dogs no more than two years old. The "Qualifying" is for dogs of all ages, provided they have never placed or earned a JAM in the Open or Amateur stake or taken two first places in previous Qualifying stakes. The "Amateur" stake is for all retrievers, provided they are handled by amateurs. The "Open" stake is for all retrievers and all handlers.

The Open and the Amateur stakes are called "major" stakes because championship points are awarded to the placing dogs. The Qualifying and the Derby are called "minor" stakes because no points are awarded.

In each stake the two judges set up a series of tests and run each competing dog through each test one after another. While the judges may run as many tests (or "series") as they need to determine a winner, they normally need only four: two by land and two by sea.

Whether on land or in water, there are two kinds of tests: "marks" and "blinds."

A "mark" (or "marking test" or "marked retrieve") is a test in which the retriever, sitting at his handler's side, sees one or more birds fall and is sent to retrieve them

The "guns" shoot a flying rooster pheasant in a field trial.

one at a time. A "single mark" (or "single") is a test in which only one bird is used—a rarity in any field trial stake. A "double mark" (or "double") is a test in which two different birds fall in different area of the field. And so on through "triples," "quads," and "quints."

A field trial test, with the handler (white jacket) waiting as the judge signals the "guns" to put the first bird in the air.

A "blind retrieve" (or more simply a "blind") is a test in which a bird is planted but the dog is not allowed to see it. His handler uses whistle and arm signals to direct ("handle") the animal to the bird. There are single, double, triple (and so on) blinds. A "cold" blind is run alone, not in conjunction with marked retrieves. A mixed test has one or more marks plus one or more blinds.

In the Derby stake, which is for younger dogs, only marks are allowed. Normally the judges will run two land doubles and two water doubles. Occasionally, they will set up a triple.

In the other three stakes, both marks and blinds are required. Typically, the judges will run a land marking test, a land blind test, a water marking test, and a water blind test. The marks may be double, triple, or quad—quints haven't been tried yet to my knowledge, but they will be. The blinds may be single, double, or triple, and may be run cold or mixed with marks. The tests in the Qualifying stake are less demanding than those in the Amateur; those in the Amateur are less demanding than those in the Open.

Each stake is an elimination contest, in that the judges set up the first test, evaluate the performance of each entered handler/dog team in turn, and then "call back" for the next test only those dogs that satisfactorily completed the first. Dogs not called back are dropped from further competition. Then the judges set up the second test and run the called-back handler/dog teams, and so on. Time limitations combined with the large entries demand severe cutting—typically one-third to one-half of the dogs—after each test. No matter how many dogs are entered, only about eight complete all the tests; the rest are dropped along the way. While this discourages many beginners, I know one determined individual who hung in there even though he didn't make it to the second series until his thirty-fourth trial!

The titles, Field Champion (FC) and Amateur Field Champion (AFC), are the major objective of serious field trialers, those who compete in the major stakes. To become an FC, a retriever must win 10 "points" in the Open stake, with at least one first place placement. To become an AFC, a retriever must win 15 points in the Amateur and/or Open stakes with an amateur handler, with at least one first. Points are awarded as follows: first place-5; second-3; third-1; fourth-½. The Open stake is for all retrievers and all handlers. The Amateur stake is for all retrievers but is limited to amateur handlers. Generally, the pro trainer runs the dog in the Open and the dog's owner runs him in the Amateur—professionally trained *dogs* run in both the Open and the Amateur.

Typically, about fifty retrievers compete in each Open and Amateur stake. Thus, placing among the top four (and thereby earning some points) constitutes a major success. Earning either dreamed-of title justifies a major celebra-

tion for both owner and pro—and perhaps an annual renewal forever after.

Not only do many dogs compete in every trial, but also the steadily rising quality of those dogs contributes significantly to the difficulty of placing. You see, there are two annual national championship trials, the National Open and the National Amateur. The dog that wins the National Open becomes a National Field Champion (NFC) and the dog that wins the National Amateur becomes a National Amateur Field Champion (NAFC). Both titles are prestigious, highly sought by those who own the best retrievers in the game. To qualify for the nationals a retriever must earn seven points in regular trials during the year: seven in the Open stakes for the National Open, and seven in the Amateur or Open stakes with an amateur handler for the National Amateur. Thus the titled dogs (FCs and AFCs) continue to compete in regular trials as long as they are physically able because their owners hope to win a national title (or another national title). Frequently, over half of the fifty or so dogs entered have already earned their FC and AFC titles. Sometimes a few of them have won previous national championships.

Since these old campaigners continue to run trial after trial, year after year, and since the judges must eliminate one-third to one-half of the dogs after each series if they hope to complete their stake in the time allotted (a day and a half), judges continually invent new, more challenging tests. In field trials, the judges possess almost total freedom to set up tests they feel will allow them to evaluate "the relative merits" of the entered dogs. Tests get longer, more complex, with more hazards (cover, terrain variations, etc.) every year. Old long-forgotten tests are revived. The professional trainers must get their dogs

A Golden delivers a bird at a trial.

through this challenging maze of tests reasonably often to make a living, so they train longer, harder, and smarter. Thus, the judges and the trainers are waging a continuous war of wits just to survive in their respective roles. The competition gets stiffer every year.

Stiff competition translates directly to cost. According to my own rough statistics, each FC or AFC point costs about $200 in entry fees alone—the cheapest part of competing. Toss in the cost of travel and training, plus the cost of dogs that never make it to their first trial (estimated at up to 90 percent, and you will have no trouble understanding why Mr. Average Retriever Owner needs some other way to exhibit his dog's talents.

Besides, the time required for serious trialing prevents participation by the work-a-day middle class. Each trial is a three-day affair, Friday through Sunday. Add two days for travel, and you see that each trial burns up a five-day "weekend." To compete successfully a person needs to enter at least twenty trials a year (thirty would be better) just to keep up on how tests are changing. How many salaried folks can devote twenty to thirty five-day weekends per year to any hobby?

Field trials produce wonderful dogs, dogs so accustomed to oh-my-god tests that they can ho-hum their way through an ordinary day's hunting, whether in the duck blind, the goose pit, or the uplands. True, field trial tests have become highly stylized, so that they no longer bear any surface reemblance to actual hunting—the handlers wear white jackets; all tests start with the handler standing and the dog sitting at heel, the handler never holds a gun, the people who throw the birds for marked retrieves wear white for greater visibility—but they still produce outstanding hunting dogs by anyone's measure. Any retriever that succeeds in the Open or Amateur stake will be a stem-winder in ordinary hunting. Even a solid Qualifying stake dog will lap the field of most "hunting" dogs that aren't trialed.

However, the money and time required for serious field trialing prevent about 90 percent of American retriever owners from participating. In other words, field trials are fantastic for those who can afford to play, but the rest of us need a game of our own.

WORKING CERTIFICATE TESTS

Most of the national breed clubs have sponsored their own non-competitive field tests for many years. These tests were designed to allow those whose primary interest is conformation (dogs show competition) to demonstrate

Field trials are competitive—and the ladies (human and canine) do their share of winning.

that their breeding stock possesses good hunting instincts and some degree of training.

While the titles earned in working certificate tests are not recognized by any registry, they have meaning among members of the national breed clubs. Therefore, these titles have contributed significantly over the years to the national breed clubs' efforts to maintain the working ability of show dogs.

All working certificate programs offer noncompetitive (pass/fail) tests, run in field trial format, in which every dog that succeeds only once receives the title. Beyond those general similarities, each national breed club has its own program, its own titles, its own requirements, and conducts its own tests.

At the low end, The Labrador Retriever Club, Inc. (LRC), has only one level of test: the working certificate (WC). In it a dog need only retrieve two short (40-yard) land single marks and two short (20- to 30-yard) water marks (steadiness and deliver to hand are not required) to earn the working certificate, which entitles the owner to place the letters "WC" after the dog's name. Members of LRC do not place a conformation championship title before a dog's name until the animal has earned a WC.

The Golden Retriever Club of America (GRCA) has a more challenging program. There are two levels: working certificate (WC), and working certificate excellent (WCX). To earn the WC title, the dog must complete a wide-spread 40- to 45-yard land double marked retrieve in moderate cover plus two water singles of about the same length. The WC doesn't require steadiness or delivery to hand. To earn the WCX title, the dog must complete a wide-spread land triple in moderate cover with the falls varying from 40- to-100 yards, plus do a simple water

double mark with an "honor" (sit off-lead while another dog works). The WCX requires steadiness and delivery to hand.

The American Chesapeake Club runs the most comprehensive working certificate program of all. There are three levels: working dog (WD), working dog excellent (WDX), and working dog qualified (WDQ). The WD is similar to the Labrador WC, requiring only two short land single marks and two short water single marks (without steadiness or delivery to hand). The WDX is almost as demanding as the GRCA WCX, requiring a long land single mark (100 yards) in medium to heavy cover, a wide-spread land double mark (50- and 75-yards) in medium cover, a long water single mark (75 yards), and a wide-spread water double mark (40- and 60-yards). The WDX also requires steadiness and delivery to hand. The WDQ is the most demanding of any working certificate test, requiring a long land double mark (90- and 130-yards) in medium cover, an 80-yard land blind retrieve with some sort of obstacle, a combination land and water triple mark with two falls in the water at 40- and 20-yards and one on land at 80 yards, and a 50- to 70-yard water blind, blind retrieve. Of course, steadiness and delivery to hand are necessary. A WDQ Chesapeake Bay Retriever is a dog any hunter would be proud to shoot over, believe me.

The other national breed clubs have working certificate programs that fall within the difficulty range described above.

Each national breed club conducts tests from time to time around the country to allow owners to earn these titles for their dogs. All such tests are non-competitive. Every dog which satisfactorily completes all the required tests

A view from behind the line at a GRCA Working Certificate test.

receives the appropriate certificate and is thereafter allowed to have the appropriate letters placed after his name. The dog need pass the tests only once to receive the title.

Working certificate tests satisfy another small group of retriever owners: those who concentrate their time and money on dog show competition, which is also expensive and time-consuming. However, just as field trials are too demanding for the many thousands of retriever-owning hunters, working certificate tests are too simple, at least for Labradors (the most popular breed). Thus, there has long been a void where the majority of retrieverites fit.

HUNTING RETRIEVER TESTS

From the time the middle class discovered retrievers, they have found nothing in their price/time range on the menu of formal off-season activities. Hunting season lasts only through fall and early winter in most states, leaving eight or nine months of inactivity for the retriever owner who doesn't fit into field trials or working certificate tests. Frustrating. Many such owners tried one thing and another. They started "Hunter" or "Gun Dog" stakes within the framework of the local retriever club's fun trials. Many tried the Qualifying stake at licensed trials. Trouble was, a guy couldn't put any kind of title on his dog either way. And titles mean a lot to all of us, no matter how we may pooh-pooh any suggestion that they do.

This frustration has grown in direct proportion to the increasing number of middle class hunters who have bought retrievers over the past twenty years. Over 100,000 retriever pups have been registered with AKC every year for some time now, so we are talking about a lot of frustrated people by 1983 when the hunting retriever movement exploded (there is no other word for it) within our long-sedate retriever world. The resoundingly enthusiastic and nationwide response to this movement's promise of meaningful, affordable, noncompetitive titles for *hunting* retrievers should have-astounded no one.

Really, there is nothing original in the hunting retriever test concept. AKC obedience trials, which always have had a wide middle class following, have used it since the 1930s. As a matter of fact, I ended my book, *Retriever Training Tests,* (which was written in early 1982, before the hunting retriever movement started) with a plea for a field testing program following the obedience trial format: non-competitive with three progressive levels, each requiring multiple successful passing efforts to earn the related title, and written descriptions of the test requirements. While not modelled directly on obedience trials, the format that has been implemented in hunting retriever tests contains the same essential elements. (Much to my surprise, I must admit, and not because of anything I wrote in that book. In fact, it didn't

Camo (or other dark clothing) is required at hunting tests.

Handlers are required to point a shotgun in hunting tests.

A "walk-up" test, in which the handler heels his dog until the bird flushes.

hit the street until the fall of 1983, by which time hunting retriever tests were in the experimental stages.)

How does this format make these tests suit the majority of retriever-owning hunters?

Most important, the fact that they are non-competitive makes them affordable. Think about it. The judges do not have to find a winner; therefore they don't have to develop harder and harder tests to "separate" (and eliminate) dogs. If every dog entered passes all the tests, wonderful! Because they don't have to find a winner, judges do not need much latitude in setting up tests. The rules can (and do) specify both minimum and maximum requirements. Therefore, the folks who enter their dogs face no significant surprises. A person can be reasonably confident that, once he trains his dog to the appropriate level, he can earn the related title in the minimum number of tests, or perhaps one or two more (dogs are always unpredictable). For example, if the rules say a dog must pass the tests at a certain level five times, the owner can plan on qualifying his dog for that particular title in five to seven attempts. Field trialers, on the other hand, may chase those elusive "points" through twenty trials a year for five years and never get enough because the competition beats them too often.

Since there are three progressive levels, the average hunter can participate as his retriever grows and develops from puppy to finished performer. He can begin running his dog when he is just beginning formal training, and continue long after he is a finished performer if he wishes.

The written requirements for each level are specific enough to be used as a training program outline. Unlike the field trialer, who knows only in the vaguest terms what will be expected in a particular trial, the hunting test handler understands in considerable detail what he and his dog will have to do to succeed each time he enters. He can prepare for specific requirements—and those requirements closely match what he should train his dog to do for actual hunting.

The successful dog earns meaningful titles. These identify the animal's precise level of accomplishment for breeders, puppy buyers, other hunters, and that segment of the general population that is familiar with retriever work. These titles also constitute a source of pride for the owner, particularly the owner/trainer.

This format encourages people to train their own dogs since the requirements are not beyond the average person's time and talent limits. While professional trainers certainly have a place in the hunting retriever world, they will never dominate it. Ordinary hunters who choose to train their own can succeed. They won't get caught in the escalating cross-fire between professional trainers and judges as they would in field trials.

The format selected for hunting retriever tests, therefore, nicely suits the majority of retriever owners, just as a similar format in obedience trials has long suited the majority of purebred pet owners who want demonstrably well-trained dogs.

At this time there are three organizations sponsoring separate (but very similar) forms of hunting tests: the AKC; the Hunting Retriever Club, which is affiliated with UKC (HRC/UKC); and the North American Hunting Retriever Association (NAHRA), which has no registry affiliations. All three sponsor tests which feature the elements described above as essential to a good program. The AKC tests are conducted all over the country by AKC-affiliated retriever clubs, many of which also conduct field trials. HRC/UKC tests are conducted around the country by the relatively new clubs which have been formed for that specific purpose. NAHRA tests are conducted by similar newly-formed clubs. Both HRC/UKC and NAHRA rely on individual memberships as well as club memberships for support.

All three organizations offer three graduated levels (like stakes) of non-competitive testing. The similarities outweigh the differences, so I will describe them together, identifying the small differences as I go along.

The lowest level, which is for dogs with little formal training, is called "Junior" by AKC, "Started" by HRC/UKC and NAHRA. This level requires only short single marked retrieves on both land and water. The dog need not be steady, nor must he deliver to hand.

The middle level, which is for reasonably well-trained retrievers, is called "Senior" by AKC, "Seasoned" by HRC/UKC, and "Intermediate" by NAHRA. This level requires double marks on land and in water, plus a very short blind retrieve in water. Steadiness and delivery to hand are mandatory. In addition to the above basics, each organization has its own unique requirements. AKC specifies a very short blind retrieve on land and a walkup test (in which the dog walks at heel until a bird is flushed and shot). HRC/UKC requires a very short land blind, a "diversion retrieve," in which a bird is shot while the dog returns with another bird, and a choice of any of the following: a walk-up, trailing, or quartering (working in front of a walking hunter to flush birds). NAHRA requires both trailing and quartering.

The highest level, which is for the fully-trained retriever, is called "Master" by AKC, "Finished" by HRC/UKC, and 'Senior" by NAHRA. This level requires significant multiple marks (doubles or triples) and blind retrieves on land and water. Steadiness and delivery to hand are mandatory. In addition to the above basics, each organization has its own unique requirements. AKC specifies that one of the blind retrieves shall be a double blind, that one of the marking tests shall be a walk-up, and that each dog shall honor another's work. HRC/UKC specifies a diversion retrieve and an honor. NAHRA specifies that one of the blind retrieves be mixed with marks, and requires both trailing and quartering.

In addition to these basic three-level tests, HRC/UKC and NAHRA periodically conduct special, higher level tests.

The HRC/UKC conducts "Grand Hunting Retriever Championship" tests for dogs which already have earned the title from their "Finished" level tests. These are more demanding tests, intended for the dogs and handlers that want to participate at an even higher level. This includes multiple marks on land and in water with diversion birds, land and water blinds which may or may not be mixed with marks, trailing, and quartering. Distances may be as much as 200 yards on land and 150 yards in water, and tests are more difficult throughout.

NAHRA conducts an annual "National Invitational" test for the dogs that have earned the most points in the highest level of their tests during the year. Dogs which successfully complete this national are named to the NAHRA "All American Team."

The most confusing difference among the three testing organizations lies in the way they award titles.

AKC offers three titles: "Junior Hunter" (JH), for the dog that successfully completes the lowest level tests on four separate occasions; "Senior Hunter" (SH) for the dog that successfully completes the middle level tests on five separate occasions; and "Master Hunter" (MH) for the dog that successfully completes the highest level tests on six separate occasions. These titles are placed *after* the dog's name, since it is the AKC custom to place competitive titles before and non-competitive titles after the name.

HRC/UKC offers three titles: 'Hunting Retriever" (HR) for the dog that earns a total of 20 championship "points" (5 points for passing the lowest level [allowed only once], 15 points for passing the midle level [allowed only once], and 20 points for passing the highest level [allowed five times]); "Hunting Retriever Champion" (HR. CH.) for the dog that earns a total of 100 championship points, with at least 80 coming in the highest level tests; "Grand Hunting Retriever Champion" (GR.HR. CH.) for the dog that wins a total of 100 grand championship points (25 points for passing the grand level [allowed 4 times]). All HRC/UKC titles are placed *before* the dog's name.

NAHRA offers two titles: "Working Retriever" (WR) for the dog that earns 20 "points" (2.5 for passing the lowest level tests [maximum of 5 points allowed]; 5 for passing the middle level [maximum 20 allowed]; 20 for passing the highest level which has no limit on total points; "Master Hunting Retriever" (MHR) for the dog that earns 100 points with at least 80 points earned in the highest level tests. NAHRA titles are placed *before the dog's name*.

So much for the essentials of hunting retriever tests. They also have a culture of their own, a "like-hunting" culture that has grown up largely as a reaction to the *perceived* non-hunting culture of field trials. Hunting retriever test afficionados never tire of explaining that everything they do is "just like hunting, not like field trials."

As you may have guessed, a new movement that already has split three ways did not float in on a blanket of olive branches. This movement saw more combat in its first three years than most hobby movements suffer in fifty years. The initial onslaught, which was probably necessary to stimulate enough nationwide emotion to establish the movement, was directed at field trials. But not at the expense involved. While that is the real issue, and while it does indeed carry a heavy emotional load, it doesn't make palatable slogans. Americans hate to whisper, let alone scream, "I can't afford it!" Another rallying cry had to be developed, one the many middle class retriever owners in this country could take pride in.

Thus was born the spurious accusations that field trials have moved completely away from hunting, and therefore that they no longer produce good hunting retrievers. The truth is that while field trials look little like ordinary hunting—which gives credence to detractors—field trials demand so much more than ordinary hunting that successful field trial dogs are unbelievably *overqualified* for hunting, rather than the opposite. There can be no question that field trials don't look like hunting: The handlers wear white jackets for better visibility; the retrieves are normally much longer and more difficult; duckblinds are not used; the small decoy spreads are normally placed to confuse the dog rather than to attract ducks; the handler stands with his dog sitting at heel to start each test.

Thus, "just like hunting, not like field trials" became an easy rally cry within the hunting retriever culture. Then it became a pillar on which rest the cultural (non-essential) features of the tests themselves. Some of these features are mildly useful; some are harmlessly theatrical; and a few waste time that could be better spent testing dogs.

First the mildly useful. Before the first dog runs in each test, the judges must explain "the hunting scenerio" to all handlers. This does force the judges to explain what they expect to the inexperienced handlers—a good move that will decrease in value as more people gain experience. The leaders of the movement initiated this requirement to force judges to set up "realistic hunting tests." The trouble is, anything can happen in hunting, so whatever the judges want to set up can be rationalized by some fanciful "hunting scenerio." Moreover, not every realistic hunting situation makes a good test for a retriever. Some are too simple. Others are dangerous. Many make it impossible for the judges to see the dog all the time—and "you can't judge 'em if you can't see 'em!"

Besides, the rules specify the tests to be run in considerable detail, limiting the judges' discretion to those hunting tests the sponsoring organizations deem within an acceptable range. Thus, beyond forcing the judges to explain what they expect in each test, this "hunting scenerio" thing does little good.

Occasionally, an "Uncle Remus" judge wastes too much time spinning wonderously long scenerios which fascinate him as much as they bore his captive audience. Some judges forget that the folks have gathered to test their dogs, not to listen to bedtime stories. Once, as a mild

form of protest, my co-judge and I "entertained" the handlers with a purely imaginary scenerio involving a non-existent bird (the "Scottish Red-Legged Partridge," as I recall) that exhibited all sorts of peculiar habits, required strange hunting procedures, and so on. Then, after all this nonsense (which the handlers seemed to enjoy as comic relief), we ran a very solid marking test that would have suited any of a thousand real hunting scenerios—or our fictionalized one, for that matter.

Another mildly useful "just like hunting" feature is the practice of introducing unusual gimmicks to test steadiness and control. Diversion birds, diversion shots, fly-aways, extended honors, placing the dog some distance from the handler, having the handler point a shotgun at every bird, and on and on. However, the insecure judge who needs to hear, "Boy, that's just like hunting," whispered about every test he creates, often overdoes these gimmicks. We should test steadiness and control, of course, but we should concentrate on the more important aspects of retriever work, namely marking and handling (on blind retrieves). Too much testing of steadiness and too little real marking and blind retrieve work rewards the "pig" (slow, plodding retriever).

The practice of hiding the people who throw the birds for marks is also mildly useful. A reaction to the white-clad throwers in field trials, this custom unfortunately sometimes gives the dog a far worse look at a fall than he gets in actual hunting. Nevertheless, it does test the dog's memory on multiple marks far better than can be done with visible throwers.

The rule that prevents the handler from trying to point out to the dog where the bird will appear is more than mildly useful. This should be added to field trial rules, where too much time goes down the tube after the handler arrives at the line and before he signals that he is ready.

Elaborate duckblinds are often used in hunting tests.

The requirement that everyone—judges, handlers, helpers, everyone—wear dark or camouflage clothing is "harmlessly theatrical." A reaction to the field trialer's white jacket, this rule sounds very practical, but it sometimes prevents the dog from seeing the handler's arm signals on blind retrieves. However, I have noticed that handlers usually find ways around this rule when they come to the line to run a blind retrieve. They roll up their camo sleeves to expose their white-ish arms; they pull out their handkerchiefs; they wear dark caps with white insides; they buy nearly white "desert" camo shirts. Once when I was judging, a handler pulled out his program, folded it so that a white page showed, and used that to give arm signals. As he left the line, he asked me if what he did was okay. I told him, "Sure, every duck hunter should carry a copy of *Wall Street Journal* to the blind." Realistically, we defeat the purpose of arm signals when we make them invisible, and handlers will find a way to be seen no matter what the rules say—and they should. The rules need to allow some form of visibility that can be used while hunting, like white gloves, which can be stuffed in a pocket out of sight when not being used.

The "role playing" which flows naturally from the more dramatic hunting scenerio presentations may seem harmlessly theatrical to some, but I find it embarrassing. I'm talking about the situation in which the judges assume hunting roles and try to carry it off through a simulated conversation with each handler as he approaches the line to run his dog: "Hey, ole buddy, you're late. Where you been? I already knocked a bird down, and it fell way over there in those cattails. Do you think your dog can pick it up for me?" Lots of this goes on in the name of "just like hunting", but to me it's more like two kids playing cowboys—"You be Roy Rogers and I'll be Gene Autry. Let's go get the bad guys."

Some of the "just like hunting" features contribute nothing to the dog work and waste valuable time. For example, rowing each dog/handler team out some distance in a boat proves little that couldn't be proved right next to shore. Ditto for putting out 100 decoys when only 6 of them affect the dog work. Long duck calling sequences, back and forth between one of the judges and one of the throwers, may demonstrate the judge's talent as a duck call tooter, but who really cares at a time supposedly set aside for testing retrievers?

However, the greatest time-wasters in the entire movement (in my frequently erroneous and sometimes hotly disputed opinion) are those two darlings of the NAHRA brand of tests: trailing and quartering. Please, fellow NAHRA members, read what I have to say before burning this book as heretical.

Trailing, in which the dog uses his nose to locate a bird which has been drug some distance through cover to simulate a running crippled bird, takes an unbelievable amount of time, and proves absolutely nothing. I've never

In hunting tests the handler sometimes must stay on a stool.

had a hunting dog that wouldn't do this naturally, with no training, sometimes the first time a cripple runs off. My wife once taught one of our dogs to trail our kids when they wandered from the yard. How did she do it? Just said the selected kid's name and pointed to the ground. No training procedure at all, really. All dogs can trail. Hell, the average Fox Terrier could be taught to trail a bird, or anything else, with little effort. Why waste fifteen to thirty minutes per dog in a hunting retriever test proving that retrievers can do what Fox Terriers could do?

What's more, retrievers are so seldom dropped for failing a trailing "test" that it would be more appropriate to call them "demonstrations." Every dog that finds the bird passes, whether he trailed it or just got lucky. Whenever I have suggested to a co-judge that we eliminate a dog because he didn't really trail the bird, I encounter the objection that we humans understand so little about canine scenting ability that we can't say definitely whether the dog was or was not trailing—he could just have a spectacular nose. If we can't judge it, why run it? It isn't a test; it's a demo. Besides, testing each dog chews up a big chunk of the available time.

Quartering, which takes longer per dog than trailing, has no place in retriever tests for three reasons.

First, if I were to judge this event correctly—using Springer Spaniel standards—I would have only passed one retriever that has run under me to date, and that one would have needed a little help from my kind heart. The quartering test turns into a jury-rigged demonstration more often than not. If the dog shuffles about in front of the handler a bit, doesn't run off, doesn't lift his leg on a judge, and remains steady when the bird is flushed and shot, he passes. Ground coverage? Pattern? Forget it.

Second, formal training in windshield-wiper quartering has a negative impact on blind retrieve training. It is extremely difficult—not impossible, granted—to teach a dog both to quarter in front of a walking hunter and also to run long straight lines and casts on blind retrieves. Since blind retrieves are "proper" retriever work, while quartering is "make-do" work at best, I feel that we should concentrate on the former.

Third, a retriever trained in proper retriever work, especially blind retrieves, muddles through in actual hunting as a flush dog without any formal training. If he understands a release command, a come-in whistle, and a stop whistle, any retriever can be taught to hunt satisfactorily in the uplands without quartering. The release command frees the dog to hunt as his instincts and experience dictate. The other two commands keep him close to the hunter. I have hunted this way for years with retrievers, and see no advantage in formal quartering for these dogs.

So much for the many "just like hunting" features of the new hunting retriever tests. Their values vary from slightly above zero to slightly below. None fall in the "essential" class. They are "just like hunting" cultural practices which can remain or fall into disuse with little impact on the value of the tests.

Actually, no matter what we do, we cannot make these tests "just like hunting" *to the dogs*. The dog still spends most of his time in a crate, trailer, or dog box—to be hurried out now and then to run a quick test, and then confined again. Unlike wild birds, test birds carry plenty of human and canine scent. The weather, cover, and water temperature don't even faintly resemble those of the hunting season. The general environment consisting of cars, barking dogs, people everywhere, the smells of the barbecue wagon, are foreign to any hunting situation the dog has ever encountered. *To the dog,* a hunting retriever test seems little different from a field trial. Nothing wrong with that, either, for field trials made these dogs the marvelous hunting dogs they are; so the field trial environment cannot be all that bad, even if the less discerning spectators fail to recognize its merits relative to "proper" retriever work. If the inexperienced feel more comfortable with copious "just like hunting" trappings, fine. The dogs don't care one way or the other.

The *essential* elements of the hunting retriever movement are: non-competitiveness, multi-level testing,

documented requirements, and meaningful titles. Give us those and it matters little whether we wear camo, white jackets, or shining armor; our dogs will be good hunting retrievers. For all its pointless cultural baggage and competing sponsors, the hunting retriever movement works. Thank God for it.

AKC, HRC/UKC, and NAHRA compete for our favor in this hunting retriever market, but we should not be lured into committing exclusively to any one of them. Each of us should support all three. We have nothing to gain by awarding a monopoly to any of them, for strong competition makes them more attentive to our needs. Besides, earning all of their titles constitutes a greater challenge than does earning only those of one sponsoring organization. Why would anyone want to damage this wonderful potpourri of affordable field activities by throwing in with only one of them?

Will all three succeed? Certainly the AKC program will grow steadily for many years to come. After all AKC has been *the* registry for retrievers since the early days of field trials. AKC has a nationwide infrastructure of clubs to conduct their tests from coast to coast and border to border. As a matter of fact, AKC has already found the hunting tests for retrievers so successful that they have initiated similar tests for pointing breeds and spaniels, and may extend this non-competitive testing format into the hound, working, and herding groups in the future. Yes, AKC hunting retriever tests ARE successful and will continue to succeed.

HRC/UKC also has a strong registry, one that is just beginning to gain strength among retrieverites. NAHRA lacks a registry, but seems to have determined leadership. Neither started out with a nationwide infrastructure of existing clubs as did AKC. Thus, both struggle to establish their presences in new teritories. HRC/UKC succeeds mostly in the South and Rocky Mountain states while NAHRA succeeds mostly on the two coasts. One wonders whether they wouldn't be better off as one organization. Both would have more clubs. NAHRA would have a registry. Together they would offer AKC a stronger challenge. It's probably too late now, for as their testing programs mature, minor differences seem to be solidifying into major barriers to any unification effort. Too bad. I can only hope that both grow, prosper, and continue to offer meaningful alternatives to AKC tests. Such competition is healthy, refreshing, and reassuring.

17

CLUBS FOR RETRIEVERITES

The most sociable people on Planet Earth—by both necessity and choice—are those who own retrievers. They are gregarious by necessity because it takes a lot of people to run any of the retriever-related activities described in the previous chapter (field trials, working certificate tests, and hunting retriever tests) and for the training associated with each.

They are also gregarious by choice, for to stay in retrievers very long a person must find the social side of these activities enjoyable and satisfying.

True, the waterfowl hunting in which the retriever breeds excel demands few of the social graces. Frequently, a solitary hunter with his retriever, man and dog shivering from cold and excitement, huddle together in a drafty blind on a wet and windy morning near a spread of decoys that rise and fall irregularly with the waves. Too many people, too many dogs, will ruin the hunt. Not social at all, really.

However, all the activities that retriever owners have invented to amuse themselves in the off-season (about 80 percent of the year) depend for success on large numbers of people; masses of humanity. Field trials, working certificates, hunting retriever tests, and training all require a ''supporting cast'' that rivals that of a Hollywood extravaganza. Let's count the number of people required for a basic all age retriever test, one you might see in the open or amateur stake of a field trial or in the highest level of a hunting retriever test: a triple marked retrieve with a single blind retrieve, and an ''honor.''

The marshal calls the handler to the line (starting point) where the two judges wait. That's three: marshal and two judges. But we haven't really started counting yet.

After the handler indicates that he and his dog are ready, one of the judges signals the #1 set of ''guns,'' who shoot a blank shell and throw a dead bird (duck or pheasant) in a high arc so that it lands in heavy cover, say 90 yards off to the left. There are two people in this set of ''guns,'' one that shoots (sometimes called a ''popper'') and one that throws (the ''thrower''). That brings the total supporting cast up to five—and we aren't close to through yet.

After the #1 bird is down, the judge signals to the #2 guns (popper and thrower), who toss another dead bird, say 75 yards straight out, again in cover. That brings us up to seven folks—and still counting.

After the #2 bird is down, the judge signals the #3 guns to shoot a ''flyer'' (live bird). This requires three helpers, one to throw the bird (''live thrower'') and two to shoot it (''live guns''). The total is now ten—and there are more to come.

The dog retrieves these three marked retrieves one at a time, usually in reverse order (#3, then #2, then #1). After he has done this, the handler lines the dog up for the blind retrieve, which is planted some 200 yards out, midway between #1 and #2 marks. However, a person had to ''plant the blind'' (place a dead bird where the dog is to be sent). That ''blind planter'' is the eleventh person working to allow this one dog to complete this one test. Hang on. There is another one!

After completing the blind retrieve, this dog must ''honor'' while the next dog runs the same test. Therefore, another handler and dog must participate before just one dog can do the entire test.

That is a total of twelve folks, not counting the dog's own handler, for just one test! In order to complete the trial or test in the allotted time, two stakes run concurrently (the open and qualifying Friday through Saturday morning, the amateur and derby Saturday afternoon through Sunday). Thus, there may be another twelve peo-

---

(Adapted from ''National Breed Clubs: What Do They Have To Offer?'' *Gun Dog,* November/December, 1987; and ''Retriever Folks Are Friendly,'' *Dog Fancy,* August, 1987.)

ple running another test somewhere else. Then, too, there are the miscellaneous "runners" that no human activity can survive without, and the field trial committee (five people) who make sure everything runs smoothly and all the results are properly documented. All told there may be thirty-five people working at any given time in such a trial or test. Field trials run sunup to sunset for three days and hunting tests do the same for two days. Since it is impossible to work the same thirty-five people that long without a break, there must be at least a few extra helpers around to spell them. A retriever club just never has too many people.

Fifty folks make for a comfortable trial or test. Most under-staffed clubs get by with less, but not comfortably. Working certificate tests require fewer helpers, as does training (where judges, runners, marshals, and trial committee are not needed). Nevertheless, you always need all those "guns" and "blind planters." When you need that kind of supporting cast, you can be very friendly. As one long-time field trialer used to say, "When you have retrievers, you have to love your neighbor *hard.*"

Not surprisingly, retriever people form into clubs as readily as ducks form into flocks. The remainder of this chapter will introduce you to the clubs you should know about as a new retriever owner. Join whichever ones appeal to you. You will be warmly welcomed, and you will quickly find that slogging in the swamp to throw birds and plant blinds is not all these folks do. They enjoy the human side of club activities, too.

THE NATIONAL BREED CLUBS

You may have heard that some sort of national club "sponsors your breed." The names of these clubs are as follows: Labrador Retriever Club, Inc. (LRC); Golden Retriever Club of America (GRCA); American Chesapeake Club (ACC); Flat-Coated Retriever Society of America (FCRSA); Curly-Coated Retriever Club of America (CCRCA); Irish Water Spaniel Club of America (IWSRCA); American Water Spaniel Club (AWSC); and Nova Scotia Duck Tolling Retriever Club, USA (NSDTRC-USA) as well as the Canadian NSDTR Club. For those new to a particular breed, information about national breed clubs seems a well-kept secret. So let's discuss them and what they offer the hunter.

While each club is unique, they all share a few common features. Each is a national organization of breeders and owners of one specific breed. The primary purpose of every one of them is to maintain and improve the breed, physically and functionally. Each is non-profit, supported by dues and income from their various activities. The members operate the club, and do all the work required on a volunteer basis. In short, these are national "hobby clubs." The members take their breed seriously, but since funds are always tight, they seldom advertise their clubs.

Seven of the eight breed clubs are affiliated with AKC. The Nova Scotia Duck Tolling Retriever has not yet received AKC recognition, although it is recognized by UKC. In Canada, where the Toller is recognized by the Canadian Kennel Club (CKC), the breed club is a CKC affiliate.

Knowledgeable breeding—breeding which preserves and improves the breed's conformation and working ability—is the primary concern of each national breed club. If the average hunter can buy a hunting retriever with reasonable assurance that he will look and act like the breed he represents, that hunter has the national breed club to thank, directly or indirectly.

First, let's review what these clubs do toward assuring that the breed looks as it should. I realize that it is bad form to admit among hunters that I enjoy the appearance of a dog which closely resembles the ideal of his breed. However, we are unfortunately in an age when we spend much more time looking at our dogs (in the kennel, by the fireplace, on the seat beside us in the truck, at the training grounds, wherever) than we do hunting them, so I will cautiously allow that I like to gaze on one that is nicely put together.

The national breed club maintains the writen AKC-approved "standard" of physical perfection for the breed and encourages breeders to strive toward it. Dog show judges use this standard as the basis for evaluating the competing dogs. "Conformation" has become a synonym for "dog show" because the dogs are judged on how closely they conform to the breed standard. Other common synonyms are "bench" and "breed."

Unfortunately, the competitiveness of dog shows has led many non-retriever breeds through various physical fads that have nothing to do with functionality: too much coat, exaggerated slope on the topline, flashy rather than efficient movement, and so forth. This same competitiveness has led to barbering and grooming that make caricatures of some of the non-retriever breeds we see in dog shows. While some of this nonsense may be creeping into the Golden Retriever fancy today, it has not significantly affected any of the other retriever breeds. Maintaining good functional physical type is important, and the national breed clubs do as good a job of this as possible, given the dog show rules under which they must operate. They would do a better job if AKC offered a noncompetitive format for evaluating conformation, similar to their obedience trial and hunting tests formats. That would eliminate most of the breeding and grooming faddishness while maintaining proper evaluation of functional conformation. It will come, too, just as have the noncompetitive field activities.

Naional breed clubs are equally intent on maintaining the working qualities of their breeds. Each one sponsors its own form of working certificate testing program, described in the chapter on field activities. Serious conformation breeders use these programs to evaluate the working ability of their show stock. Owners and breeders primarily interested in field activities and hunting sometimes run their dogs in these tests just because "they are there." While working certificate tests require significantly less than field trials and hunting tests, they do contribute to breed improvement.

Perhaps the most visible benefit of membership in a national breed club is the newsletter that each of them, except the LRC, publishes. These newsletters are written and edited by members who are typically paid nothing. Amateurs, you might call them, if you keep in mind that the original meaning of the word was "one who loves."

What are these newsletters like? Well, they vary so much in size, format, frequency, and content that it is impossible to describe a "typical" one, so let's take a look at a couple of examples.

Golden Retriever News is a BIG newsletter, running over 130 pages each bi-monthly issue, in magazine-size format. Some of this bulk is due to the large amount of paid advertising—an enviable situation for any national breed club—but it also runs complete coverage of conformation, obedience, tracking, and field, with an editor for each activity assisting the one overall editor. *GRNEWS* also carries many feature articles and short columns from all the local and regional clubs associated with GRCA. With plenty of black and white photos throughout, this is the Cadillac of national breed club newsletters. It has won many awards for its excellence.

The American Water Spaniel Club Newsletter is a small but excellent newsletter. Published quarterly on 16 by 11 inch newspaper stock, with just 4 pages, it contains very complete coverage of conformation and obedience, as well as field.

The newsletters of the other breed clubs fall somewhere within the range of those two, except, as I mentioned above, LRC, which does not publish a newsletter.

Most national breed clubs also support a network of affiliated local and regional clubs which promote the national club's aims and activities at the backyard level. Membership in such a local club constitutes a major benefit for members of the national group.

Let me pose a question: Which do you REALLY enjoy more—working with your retrievers or discussing them with other dog folks? Most people will answer that it depends; sometimes one and sometimes the other. When your dog is having a problem, you first and foremost want to work it out, but after you do that, you probably find it nice to have someone who will listen while you (modestly) describe your clearly ingenious and deft handling of the entire matter. And if that someone, after respectfully listening to your wisdom for at least thirty minutes, wishes to bore you with his mundane solution to a trivial problem for another thirty minutes, you are always magnanimous enough to listen, right?

If you fit the above description, you belong in a local breed club. They are scattered around the country for most

Field trial gallery at a national specialty.

breeds, to satisfy this strong social need, and they are normally associated with the national breed clubs. Join the national and you are welcome in the local, and vice versa.

However, local breed clubs affiliated with the nationals are more than social groups. They are, along with the national newsletter, the communications link between the national club and the individual member. They are the vehicles by which national programs are carried out. They are the testboards for new programs. They are the hosts for established activities.

Local breed clubs conduct the working certificate tests; they hold the national specialties and the regional specialties; they act as host club for whatever activity the national club wishes to sponsor. If the national wants to experiment with a new activity, it will do this through a willing local breed club. When the national is looking for new leadership, it will look first to those who have been successful in local club leadership—makes sense, doesn't it?

Besides, local breed clubs are fun for the members. Fun trials, fun conformation matches, practice obedience trials—"picnics and hay rides and mid-winter sleigh rides."

But the national breed clubs offer still more.

The mountain men had their annual "rendezvous"; college and high school classes have their reunions; entertainment media have their annual award shows; not surprisingly then, national breed clubs have their annual "national specialties" which are a combination rendevous, reunion, and award show.

The typical national specialty lasts about a week and consists of a field trial, a hunting retriever tests, a working certificate test, an obedience trial, a tracking test, an endless array of complicated conformation classes, meetings, meetings, meetings, parties, parties, parties, with ample opportunities for miscellaneous socializing in between—followed by at least three day's sleep when you get home.

If you go to just one, you will return again and again, and never even wonder why. You will see the best dogs from all over the continent compete in conformation, obedience, tracking, and field, and you will enjoy even those whose area of specialization isn't your own. You will see people you only see once a year, and wish you could see more often.

How does one go about joining a national breed club? Well, each of them has its own rules, and they all come off very pompous and restrictive—you know, "must be recommended by two members in good standing and accepted by the full board sitting . . ." Actually, it is much more democratic than it sounds, and if you are a tolerably decent sort, you will have no trouble joining. There are different classes of membership in some clubs: family, single, junior, and senior citizen. The cost runs from $5

to about $30 per year, and that includes the newsletter. Pretty cheap, really.

Appendix II contains the name and address of a contact for each of the eight national breed clubs.

RETRIEVER FIELD TRIAL CLUBS, HUNTING TEST CLUBS

These are the local and regional organizations which conduct the field trials and hunting tests discussed in the previous chapter. They come in three flavors: AKC, HRC/UKC, and NAHRA.

AKC-affiliated retriever clubs operate in all large and many medium-sized cities in the country. They make up the field trial infrastructure that accepted the hunting retriever test movement (with more or less grace) and made these new AKC tests widely available. True, some clubs have not accepted the hunting test movement, and a few of these probably never will. However, most of the established field trial clubs, always hungry for more workers at their trials, gladly embraced hunting tests because of the potential for increased membership. AKC publishes a bi-monthly, tabloid-type newsletter, *The Hunter's Whistle,* which you will find quite helpful.

HRC/UKC retriever clubs have operated just during the short history of the hunting test movement. Strong in Louisiana duck hunting country and through the Rocky Mountain states, especially Colorado, these clubs are spreading gradually through the midlands, too. The UKC has long been THE registry for coonhounds, as well as for several breeds not recognized by AKC. In recent years, UKC has taken aggressive action to broaden its area of influence, primarily in obedience trials and hunting retriever tests. Having a respected registry behind it certainly lends strength to the HRC/UKC brand of hunting tests. The structure for maintaining all the related records was in place before the first "hunt" (as they call their tests). Individuals as well as clubs can join HRC/UKC. Individual members receive the bi-monthly magazine, *Hunting Retriever,* a slick-paper publication which has been a winner in the Dog Writers Association of America annual awards program.

NAHRA retriever clubs have operated only since the start of the hunting retriever movement. Very strong on the East Coast and growing strong on the West Coast, NAHRA also has clubs scattered through the Midwest. Since NAHRA has no registry, it has had to establish its own record-keeping mechanism. NAHRA also offers individual memberships, providing those who join with a quarterly magazine, *NAHRA News.*

Anyone interested in hunting retriever tests should contact all three parent organizations to locate the nearest affiliated local or regional club. HRC/UKC and NAHRA will also happily provide information on individual

An outdoor dog show at a national specialty.

memberships in the national clubs. The addresses are in Appendix II.

If you are fortunate enough to have all three types of clubs in your area, join them all! The tests are sufficiently similar that a dog trained for one of them will need only minor additional training to pass the other two.

These local clubs typically have many activities besides the formal trials and tests. Some have monthly practice trials (also called fun trials and picnic trials). Some have training classes, especially for new members. Most have land and water leased, where members can train (and perhaps hunt and fish). They all have the usual array of social activities.

THE OBEDIENCE TRAINING CLUB

While almost every medium- to large-sized community in the country has at least one obedience training club, most retriever-owning hunters go through life without realizing what a magnificent resource these clubs are. Too bad.

Of course, the primary purpose of such an organization is to conduct licensed obedience trials and formal obedience trial competition; most retrieverites just don't have the time, energy, and money for another activity like that. While advanced obedience exercises are challenging enough to be a sport in themselves (jumping, retrieving dumbbells, scent work, etc.) the basic stuff (HEEL, SIT, DOWN, STAY, COME) are essential for the hunting retriever, whether he ever enters the obedience trial ring

or not. What's more, most of these clubs offer to the general public a beginner's course in basic obedience.

In these courses groups of inexperienced owners learn how to train their own dogs under the supervision of experienced volunteer club members. Normally, such a course costs $25 to $50 and lasts 9 to 12 weeks, with a weekly 1-hour class. Between classes each owner is expected to train his own dog at home every day.

Obedience clubs conduct these classes for a number of reasons. First, it brings in new members who will become involved in formal obedience trials. In fact, membership in the club usually requires successful completion of the introductory course. Second, it is good public relations within the community, for the club, and for every responsible dog owner in the area. Third, since this course makes practical training techniques available to all area dog owners, it is a public service.

Retriever-owning hunters who have never trained a dog should certainly investigate this easy and quick way to learn how to teach their dogs basic obedience. The hunting retriever must understand HEEL, SIT, DOWN, STAY, and COME before he can be gainfully employed in his life's work. What better way for the inexperienced owner to learn how to instill this basic obedience than under the tutelage of instructors who specialize in such training as their major hobby interest?

There are two kinds of obedience trials, and hence two kinds of clubs. Most trials and most clubs are affiliated with AKC, but there is a growing number of UKC trials and clubs. Either will do nicely for the retriever owner. To find the club closest to you, contact both AKC and UKC. Both addresses are in Appendix II.

THE LOCAL KENNEL CLUB

These clubs conduct the AKC dog shows that carry such an unjustifiably bad reputation among hunting dog owners. Most of those who damn conformation have never been to a dog show, have no idea what their purposes are, but have long been convinced that conformation is somehow responsible for all the ills his breed has ever suffered.

Nonsense. Conformation folks are as devoted to their dogs as we hunters are to ours—maybe more so, when you consider the time they spend bathing and grooming them. These people are determined to preserve and improve "type" in their breeds: that is, to keep the physical appearance of the breed what it is supposed to be, according to the written standard. They do this by competing in dog shows and breeding those dogs which win consistently.

Your first trip to a dog show will confuse you about the place of conformation in the real world, just as your first trip to a field trial will confuse you about the place of trials in the hunting world. Both are highly esoteric competitons, difficult to understand and easy to criticize. Both work nicely, but neither appears rational to the uninitiated.

Explaining the mechanics of dog shows is beyond the scope of this book (there are plenty of other books that do that better than I could) but I have included this brief section about them for a couple of reasons.

First, I want to encourage those who appreciate a good-looking representative of their chosen breed to attend a few local dog shows, talk to some of the exhibitors, and learn the place conformation occupies in the world of purebred dogs. If our retrievers look somewhat like the breeds they are supposed to be, we have dog shows to thank. True, not every hunter cares what his dog looks like, as long as he works as he should, but there are many who appreciate a good-looking dog—even though our hunting culture has conditioned us to deny such "affectations."

Second, I believe we could have true dual-purpose retrievers—field and conformation—if we had a non-competitive dog show format similar to our new non-competitive hunting test format. The competition in dog shows makes that sport expensive, too—not as much so as field trials, but costly enough to preclude most dedicated dog show exhibitors from entering serious field activities, too. If there were a non-competitive conformation title available, that would no longer be true. Serious breeders could finally develop the dual-purpose dogs they have only paid lip service to for decades, especially in the more popular breeds (Labrador, Golden).

In early 1982 I ended my book, *Retriever Training Tests,* with a wish that we could have non-competitive field titles. It was a pipe-dream of mine, since such a thing was not being seriously considered at that time. However, surprise, surprise. By the time the book was actually published, in late 1983, non-competitive field tests were up and running—not because I had wished it, but because its time had come.

While I am really not superstitious, I am closing this book with a similar wish—that AKC will soon offer non-competitive conformation titles—in the fond hope that the same *post hoc ergo propter hoc* sequence will procede from this wish.

The obedience trial at a national specialty.

88

APPENDIX I

Glossary of Hunting Retriever Terms

AMATEUR FIELD CHAMPION (AFC): an AKC title awarded to a retriever that wins a total of 15 points in the Amateur stakes at licensed field trials or 10 points in the Open stake with an amateur handler, or 15 points with an amateur handler from any combination of Open and Amateur stakes. At least 5 points must come from a first place win.

AMATEUR STAKE: the stake at AKC-licensed field trials in which all dogs must be handled by amateurs. It is a "major" stake because points toward the AFC title are awarded to the four placing dogs. Five points go to the first place dog. Three to the second place dog. One point to the third place dog. One-half point to the fourth place dog.

AMERICAN KENNEL CLUB (AKC): This is the largest all-breed registry in the country. It has been the major register for retrievers almost from the beginning. Located in New York, it sponsors dog shows, obedience trials, tracking tests, field trials, and hunting tests.

ARM SIGNALS: When a handler wishes to redirect his retriever when the dog is moving some distance from him (normally on a blind retrieve but sometimes on a mark), he stops the dog with a whistle signal and waves his arm in the approprite direction. This is also called "casting," and it is a major part of blind retrieves.

BENCH: This term is a synonym for "dog show" or "conformation" or "breed." All refer to dog show competition. This term derives from the fact that it was once the custom at dog shows to keep all entered dogs on public display throughout the day on "benches."

BLIND: There are three possible meanings for this word in hunting retriever circles (an economy of words we can scarcely afford!).

First, it can mean "blind retrieve," the type of retrieve in which the dog does not see the bird fall, but is directed to it through whistle and arm signals.

Second, it can mean "duck blind," a form of concealment used in actual duck hunting and in the hunting tests which simulate actual hunting.

Third, it can mean the "holding blind" in which dogs and handlers wait their turn to run a test in a field trial or hunting test.

BLIND RETRIEVE: a retrieve in which the dog does not see the bird fall, so does not know where it is. The handler directs the dog to the bird through "lining," "stopping," and "casting" techniques. This involves whistle and arm signals.

BREED: Overlooking the obvious meaning of this word, namely a specific breed of dogs, such as the Labrador, consider for now only the meaning as the term is commonly used in the dog show world, where it is a synonym for "bench," "conformation," and "dog show." All refer to dog show competition. The term "breed," in this sense, derives from the fact that dogs are said to be competing in the "breed ring."

BREED SPLIT: This term denotes the situation in a specific breed of dogs, such as the Labrador or Golden, in which there are two distinct types of dogs, one for dog show competition, the other for field trials and hunting.

CASTING: This refers to the manner in which a handler gives arm and whistle signals to redirect his retriever to a bird. Normally, casting is done on a blind retrieve, but it can also be useful on a mark when the dog cannot find the bird.

CHAMPION (CH): This is the AKC conformation title which is awarded to the dog which wins a total of 15 points, with at least two "major" wins (3 to 5 points). Points awarded in each breed at each show depend on the area and the number of dogs entered in each breed.

COMPANION DOG (CD): Awarded by AKC to a dog which successfully completes the exercises in the Novice class (lowest level) at licensed obedience trials three times.

The title, "CD," is placed after the dog's name since it is a non-competitive title.

COMPANION DOG EXCELLENT (CDX): title awarded by AKC to a CD dog which successfully completes the exercises in the Open class (second level) at licensed obedience trials three times. The title, "CDX," is placed after the dog's name since it is a non-competitive title.

CONFORMATION: a synonym for "dog show," "bench," and "breed." All refer to dog show competition. The term, "conformation," derives from the fact that in dog shows, the entrants are judged on how well they "conform" to the written breed standard.

DERBY STAKE: the stake in AKC-licensed field trials which is limited to dogs that have not yet reached their second birthdays on the first day of the trial. Since no FC or AFC championship points are awarded, this is called a "minor" stake. However, *Retriever Field Trial News* maintains records of the dogs that place in the Derby and annually award a "Derby Dog of the Year" trophy.

DIVERSION: another word in which we have vested too many meanings, too much economy. It has three possible meanings.

First, in a double marked retrieve, the last bird down (normally the first retrieved) is the "diversion" bird while the first one down (normally the last retrieved) is the "memory" bird.

Second, in certain hunting tests, a "diversion" bird is thrown as the dog returns with another bird. The dog is expected to deliver the bird he carries before going after the diversion bird.

Third, a shot fired any time during a test is called a "diversion" if it is not associated with any of the marks.

DOG SHOW: a formal competition in which dogs are judged on how well they conform to the written standard of physical perfection for their respective breeds. Championship points are awarded in each breed according to the area and the number of dogs of each breed entered.

DOUBLE: a marked retrieve in which two birds are thrown, one at a time, in different areas. The dog is expected to remain steady for both, and then to retrieve them one at a time on command. Normally, the dog will retrieve the last bird thrown first, since it is freshest in his mind.

DUMMY: an artificial substitute for a bird, frequently used to train retrievers because of its easy availability and lower cost over the long haul. Dummies are always cylindrical and come in many sizes, from puppy dummies about 2 inches in diameter and 6 inches long to large ones 4 by 14 inches. Some are made of canvas stuffed with cork or other material, but the most popular are hollow plastic affairs with knobby surfaces. These plastic dummies come in a variety of colors for a variety of visibility situations.

FIELD CHAMPION (FC): title awarded by AKC to a dog which wins a total of 10 points in the Open stake at licensed field trials. Five of those points must be won by taking a first place. The points are given just as in the Amateur stake (see above).

FIELD DOG STUD BOOK (FDSB): an all breed registry in Chicago, which has long controlled pointer and setter field trials. Retrievers can be registered in FDSB, but FDSB doesn't conduct trials and tests for them.

FIELD TRIAL: A competitive event held under AKC regulations. There are four stakes: Open, Amateur, Qualifying, and Derby. Each is separately defined in this glossary.

FIELD TRIAL CLUB: A local or regional club formed to conduct AKC-licensed field trials. Many of these clubs have also assumed responsibility for conducting AKC-licensed hunting tests.

FINISHED STAKE: the name of the highest level stake in HRC/UKC hunting tests. It is similar to the "Master" stake in AKC tests and to the "Senior" stake in NAHRA tests.

FLUSHING SPANIEL BREEDS: These are those breeds recognized by AKC as "spaniels" and therefore allowed to compete in AKC-licensed spaniel field trials. The specific breeds are: English Springer, Welsh Springer, Cocker, English Cocker, Clumber, Field, and Sussex Spaniels. These breeds excel at quartering ahead of the hunter in the uplands, flushing and retrieving. They may also be used for waterfowl retrievers whenever the weather and water conditions are not too severe for their coats and body type, in other words during the early season. Just as retrievers cannot match spaniels in the uplands, spaniels cannot match retrievers in the water.

FUN TRIAL: informal, non-sanctioned trials held by many field trials clubs as practice trials for their members. This term is a synonym for "picnic trial."

GRAND HUNTING RETRIEVER CHAMPION (GR.H.R.CH.): title awarded by HRC/UKC to the dog which accumulates 100 points in the Grand Hunting Retriever stake at HRC/UKC hunts. This is the highest hunting retriever title awarded by HRC/UKC. Like all HRC/UKC titles, it goes before the dog's name.

GROUP: AKC has divided the 130 breeds it recognizes into seven "groups": sporting, hound, herding, working, terrier, toy, and non-sporting. All retrievers (as well as pointing breeds and spaniels) are classified as Sporting Group breeds. In dog shows, the Best of Breed winner for each breed competes in the "Group" for the four placements there. Then, the winner of each Group (seven dogs in all) compete for Best In Show honors.

GUN: In a field trial or hunting test, anyone who throws birds or shoots in each test is called a "gun," as sort of a generic synonym for "helper." The people who throw birds are called "throwers" as well as "guns," the people who shoot blank shells are called "poppers," and the people who shoot live ammunition at live birds are called "live guns." Sometimes the people who throw live birds are called "live throwers"; however, they will all answer to the generic name, "guns," especially at lunch time.

HAND SIGNALS: a synonym for "arm signals." It is part of "casting," which is part of "handling" a dog to a blind retrieve.

HANDLE: There are two meanings for this term (more unwanted economy).

First it is a broad term used to describe everything a person does to control and assist a retriever while training, trialing, or testing. Insofar as the person is the "handler," everything he/she does (good, bad, or indifferent) is "handling."

Second, in the more restrictive use of the word, a person only "handles" a dog when he works the animal to a blind retrieve. In other words, when he lines, stops, and casts the dog to a bird he hasn't seen fall.

HOUND BREEDS: This is another group of hunting dogs, distinct from those in the sporting groups by what they hunt and the way they go about it. Hounds hunt fur, whereas sporting dogs hunt feathers. There are two types of hounds: sight, and scent. Sight hounds (Greyhounds, Salukis, Irish Wolfhounds, etc.) hunt by hot pursuit of an animal that is in sight. Scent hounds (Beagles, Coonhounds, Foxhounds, etc.) trail animals that are not in sight.

HUNT: Overlooking the obvious—that exhilarating sport we all would prefer to what we are doing right now (especially moi!)—this word has another, more esoteric meaning in the HRC/UKC world. There it is the official name for their hunting retriever tests.

HUNTING RETRIEVER (HR): Besides bearing a striking resemblance to the title of one of my favorite books, this term constitutes the lowest level title awarded by HRC/UKC in their hunts. It is given to dogs that have succeeded in their middle level ("Seasoned") stake. Like all UKC titles, it goes before the dog's name.

HUNTING RETRIEVER CLUB (HRC): the sponsoring organization for one of the three formats of hunting retriever tests. Since it is affiliated with UKC, I normally abbreviate it HRC/UKC.

HUNTING RETRIEVER CHAMPION (H.R.CH.): title awarded by HRC/UKC to the retriever that has won 100 points in licensed hunts, at least 80 of which must come from the Finished stake. This title is placed before the dog's name, according to UKC standard practices with all titles.

HUNTING TEST: the generic name for non-competitive tests for sporting dogs. AKC sponsors separate types for retrievers, spaniels, and pointing breeds, and will probably initiate similar non-competitive events for hound, herding, and working breeds in the future.

HUNTING TEST CLUB: any club formed specifically to conduct hunting retriever tests for any of the three sponsoring organizations. They are similar to field trial clubs.

INTERMEDIATE STAKE: the name given to the middle level stake at NAHRA tests, the equivalent of the "Seasoned" stake in HRC/UKC hunts and the "Senior" stake in AKC tests.

JUDGES AWARD OF MERIT (JAM): award given in all licensed field trial stakes to those dogs which successfully complete all of the tests (or series) but fail to place. It is an "also-ran" award, but greatly appreciated in the stiff competition of licensed field trials.

JUNIOR HUNTER (JH): title awarded by AKC to the dog which successfully completes four Junior stakes (lowest level) at licensed hunting tests. Since it is a non-competitive title, it goes after the dog's name, per standard AKC practice.

JUNIOR STAKE: the lowest stake in AKC hunting tests, equivalent to the "Started" stake in HRC/UKC hunts and NAHRA tests.

KENNEL CLUB: This term usually applies to those local and regional organizations, affiliated with AKC, which conduct dog shows once or twice each year.

KENNEL RUN: This is applied loosely to any type of canine living quarters, but I hope that when you speak of your kennel runs you will only speak of the finest concrete and chain-link canine castle—which is no more than your hunting retrievers deserve, right?

LINING: the first of the three parts of a blind retrieve. The handler "lines" his retriever when he initially sends the dog from the heel position toward the bird.

LOCAL BREED CLUB: a local or regional organization, normally affiliated with a national breed club, dedicated to furthering the interests of one specific breed.

LIVE GUN: a person who, in a field trial or hunting test, shoots live birds for the dog to retrieve. Normally, these are the best skeet shots in the area, but I have judged one or two events in which the live guns must have been recruited from the area bird watching society.

MARKED RETRIEVE: any retrieve in which the dog sees the bird(s) fall and is expected to retrieve them without handler assistance.

MARK: a shortened form for "marked retrieve."

MASTER HUNTER (MH): title awarded by AKC to the dog which successfully completes the Master stake at licensed hunting tests six times. It is the highest hunting test title awarded by AKC and is placed after the dog's name since it is a non-competitive AKC title.

MASTER STAKE: the highest level stake at AKC hunting tests, equivalent to the "Finished" stake in HRC/UKC hunts and the "Senior" stake in NAHRA tests.

MASTER HUNTING RETRIEVER (MHR): title awarded by NAHRA to the dog which earns 100 points in NAHRA tests, at least 80 of which must come from the Senior stake. This is the highest title awarded by NAHRA.

MEMORY BIRD: the first bird down in a multiple marked retrieve. It is called the "memory bird" because it is normally the last bird retrieved, thereby requiring that the dog remember it while he retrieves the other bird(s).

NATIONAL AMATEUR FIELD CHAMPION (NAFC): title awarded by AKC each year to the dog which wins the annual National Amateur Championship field trial. To compete in this trial, a dog must have won 7 points in licensed field trial Amateur stakes (or 7 points in the Open stake with an amateur handler) in the 12 months preceding the National trial. In the National Amateur, the dogs are run through ten tough tests before a winner is declared. It is a great honor to even finish all tests and become a "finalist."

NATIONAL BREED CLUB: a nationwide organization of serious fanciers of one breed. This club is normally affiliated with AKC, and maintains the AKC-approved written standard of physical perfection for the breed. My personal opinion is that every owner of a hunting retriever should belong to his national breed club. It will keep him informed and involved.

NATIONAL FIELD CHAMPION (NFC): the title awarded by AKC each year to the dog which wins the annual National Championship field trial. To compete in this trial, a dog must have won 7 points in licensed field trial Open stakes in the 12 months preceding the National trial. The entrants are run through ten tough series before a winner is picked. It is a great honor to even finish all tests and become a "finalist."

NORTH AMERICAN HUNTING RETRIEVER ASSOCIATION (NAHRA): one of the three organizations which sponsor hunting retriever tests.

OBEDIENCE CLUB: In all large and many medium-sized cities there is a club devoted to formal obedience training and trialing. They offer the general public introductory courses in basic obedience training. These courses can be valuable to the first-time retriever owner.

Most of these clubs are affiliated with AKC, but some are affiliated with UKC. To find the one closest to you, contact both AKC and UKC, whose addresses are in Appendix II.

OBEDIENCE TRIAL: a formal activity for those involved in serious obedience training. Both AKC and UKC sponsor very similar trials. Both have three levels of non-competitive titles. AKC also offers a competitive title for dogs which have won all three non-competitive titles. The AKC non-competitive titles are: Companion Dog (CD), Companion Dog Excellent (CDX), and Utility Dog (UD). these are placed after the dog's name. The AKC com-

petitive title is Obedience Trial Champion (O.T.Ch.), which is placed before the dog's name. The UKC titles are: U-CD, U-CDX, and U-UD, all of which are placed before the dog's name.

OBEDIENCE TRIAL CHAMPION (O.T. CH.): the competitive obedience trial title awarded by AKC to a dog which wins 100 points in the Open and Utility classes after first earning all 3 non-competitive titles. The O.T.Ch. title is placed before the name.

OPEN STAKE: This is the stake in AKC-licensed field trials which is open to all dogs and all handlers. This is the "big" stake, the one in which points are awarded toward the FC title.

PICNIC TRIAL: a synonym for "fun trial" (see above).

PIG: This is a derogatory term for a retriever that works in a slow, disinterested manner. It is the canine equivalent of a "plug" racehorse.

POINTING BREEDS: that loose collection of breeds that have one trait in common: They all point, or "stand" their game, rather than flushing it. There are many, many different breeds that do this, and it seems that more are entering this country from somewhere every year. These are the best dogs for hunting quail and any other game bird that sits nicely for a point. Pointing breeds are not equipped for serious waterfowl retrieving in bad weather.

POPPER: This term has two meanings:

First, it is the person who fires a blank gun as a dead bird is thrown in a field trial or hunting test.

Second, it is a type of blank shotgun shell, one that has no pellets, only powder.

QUALIFYING STAKE: This is a minor stake in AKC-licensed field trials. Entries are limited to those dogs which have never placed or received a JAM in the Open or Amateur stakes or won two first places in previous Qualifying stakes. It is a minor stake because no points toward field titles can be won in it. However, a dog that places first or second in the Qualifying stake becomes a "qualified all age dog." The major significance of this status is that there must be at least twelve qualified all age dogs entered in the Open and Amateur stakes before championship points are awarded.

The Qualifying stake was put into the field trial scheme to make a place for the "meat dog" (everyday hunting dog), and before the hunting retriever movement, this stake was the only place where middle class retriever owners (like myself) could hope to compete successfully. However, placements and JAMs are a bit hollow, since they do not lead to a title of any sort. After the impact of hunting tests on the Qualifying stake has been fully assessed—and I think it will be dramatic—I look for a restructuring of field trials to bring this stake more into the mainstream by giving it a new purpose like making a placement in it a prerequisite to entry into the major stakes.

RETRIEVER BREEDS: the eight breeds covered in this book; breeds developed primarily for retrieving shot birds on land and in water, but breeds that can also do reasonably well as upland flush dogs. They lag behind the flushing spaniels in serious upland work just as the flushing spaniels lag behind retrievers in serious water-fowl retrieving.

SEASONED STAKE: the middle stake in HRC/UKC hunts. It is comparable to the ''Senior'' stake in AKC tests and to the ''Intermediate'' stake in NAHRA tests.

SENIOR HUNTER (SH): the title awarded by AKC to the dog which successfully completes the Senior (middle level) stake five times in AKC hunting tests. The title is placed after the dog's name, since AKC reserves the before-the-name position for competitively won titles.

SENIOR STAKE: the middle level stake in AKC hunting tests. It is comparable to the ''Seasoned'' stake in HRC/UKC hunts and to the ''Intermediate'' stake in NAHRA tests.

SERIES: The complete running of a single test in a field trial or hunting test stake. In each series, the judges set up a test (some combination of marks and/or blinds) and observe as each ''in contention'' handler/dog team tries to successfully complete that test. The name ''series'' derives from the fact that the handler/dog teams run the test one at a time—''in series,'' as opposed to ''in parallel.''

SINGLE: a shortened form of ''single marked retrieve,'' a retrieving test in which only one bird is thrown for the dog.

STAKE: a grouping of comparable dogs for judging purposes in field trials and hunting tests. The sponsoring organization established requirement for each stake, and handler/dog team entered must satisfy those requirements. For example, the field trial Derby stake is limited to dogs not yet two years old on the first day of the trial. The Amateur stake requires that the handler be an amateur (per current AKC rules). All handler/dog teams entered in the same stake run the same tests (until eliminated, of course) in series after series. The sponsoring organization may also establish minimum and maximum limits on the tests for any given stake. For example, NAHRA limits the length of the water blind test in their middle stake, the Intermediate, to 30 yards.

Each stake has it's own set of judges. A judge may judge more than one stake, but not at the same time. If two stakes run simultaneously, each must have separate judges.

STANDARD: This is a basis for judgement. In hunting tests, retrievers are judged against the written performance standard of the sponsoring organization (AKC,

HRC/UKC, NAHRA). In dog shows the dogs are judged on how well they conform to the written standard of physical perfection for their respective breeds.

STARTED STAKE: the lowest level stake in HRC/UKC hunts and NAHRA hunting tests. It is comparable to the ''Junior'' stake in AKC hunting tests.

STOPPING: part of the blind retrieve, along with ''lining'' and ''casting.'' After the dog has been lined toward the bird, he may drift off one way or the other. If he does, the handler blows a ''Stop'' whistle command (normally a single sharp blast), after which the dog should stop, turn to face the handler, and sit down (if on land) or tread (if in water) to await a ''casting'' whistle and/or arm signal. Good stopping is crucial to the blind retrieve, for ''you can't handle them if you can't stop them!''

TEST: a retrieving situation set up by the two judges to test the dogs running in a particular stake of a field trial or hunting test. Depending on the stake, the test can be very simple (a short, single mark) or quite complex (a triple mark with a double blind and an honor). Each handler/dog team in contention in the stake runs the entire test when called to the line to be judged (unless they fail before completing it, of course).

THROWER: a person who throws dead or live birds during a test at a field trial or hunting tests. A person who throws a live bird (a ''flier'') is sometimes called a ''live thrower.''

TRACKING: a formal AKC-sponsored sport in which dogs earn non-competitive titles by tracking human beings for considerable distances through the countryside and locating a dropped object (usually a glove) at the end of the track. There are two levels of tests: Tracking Dog and Tracking Dog Excellent.

TRACKING DOG (TD): the title awarded by AKC to a dog which successfully completes the lower level track at a licensed tracking test one time. Since it is a non-competitive AKC title, it goes after the dog's name.

TRACKING DOG EXCELLENT (TDX): the title awarded by AKC to a dog which successfully completes the higher level track at a licensed tracking test one time. Since it is a non-competitive AKC title, it goes after the dog's name.

TRIPLE: a multiple marked retrieve in which three separate birds are thrown for the dog, each bird in a separate area. The dog must wait until all three are down and then retrieve them one at a time. This tests his steadiness, his marking ability, and his memory.

TYPE: a dog show term which denotes the unique physical characteristics of a particular breed. ''Type'' is what makes a Labrador, for example, physically distinct from any of the other eight retriever breeds.

TYPEY: This is an adjective applied, in dog show circles, to a dog that possesses plenty of its breed's distinct physical characteristcs.

UKC COMPANION DOG (U-CD): the title awarded by UKC to a dog which successfully completes the exercises in the Novice class (lowest level) at UKC obedience Trials three times. Since it is a UKC title, it goes before the dog's name.

UKC COMPANION DOG EXCELLENT (U-CDX): the title awarded by UKC to a dog which successfully completes the exercises in the Open class (second level) at UKC obedience trials three times. Since it is a UKC title, it goes before the dog's name.

UKC UTILITY DOG (U-UD): title awarded by UKC to a dog which successfully completes the exercises in the Utility class (highest level at UKC obedience trials three times. Since it is a UKC title, it goes before the dog's name.

UNITED KENNEL CLUB(UKC): an all-breed registry located in Kalamazoo, Michigan. It has long the THE registry for the coonhound fancy, and has recently become active in retrievers. Together with the Hunting Retriever Club (HRC) they sponsor one of the three forms of hunting retriever tests.

UTILITY DOG (UD): title awarded by AKC to a dog which successfully completes the exercises in the Utility class (highest level) at AKC obedience trials three times. Since it is an AKC non-competitive title, it is placed after the dog's name.

WORKING CERTIFICATE (WC): title awarded by several of the retriever national breed clubs to those dogs which successfully complete a basic working certificate test one time. These tests and titles have contributed much to the maintenance of the working abilities of show stock retrievers. Since the title is non-competitive, it is placed after the dog's name.

WORKING CERTIFICATE EXCELLENT (WCX): title awarded by several of the retriever national breed clubs to those dogs which successfully complete an advanced working certificate test one time. This test and title have contributed much to the maintenance of the working ability of show stock retrievers. Since it is non-competitive, the title is placed after the dog's name.

WORKING DOG (WD): title awarded by the American Chesapeake Club to those Chesapeake Bay Retrievers which successfully complete a basic working dog test one time. This test has contributed much to the maintenance of the working ability of show stock Chesapeakes. Since it is non-competitive, the title is placed after the dog's name.

WORKING DOG EXCELLENT (WDX): title awarded by the American Chesapeake Club to those Chesapeake Bay Retrievers which successfully complete a more advance working dog test one time. This test has contributed much to the maintenance of the working ability of show stock Chesapeakes. Since it is non-competitive, the title is placed after the dog's name.

WORKING DOG QUALIFIED (WDQ): title awarded by the American Chesapeake Club to those Chesapeake Bay Retrievers which successfully complete the most advanced working dog test one time. This is the only test of this sort which requires blind retrieves, so it is highly significant in maintaining the working ability of the Chesapeake breed. Since it is non-competitive, the title is placed after the dog's name.

WORKING CERTIFICATE TEST: a testing program established and sponsored by the various national breed clubs to test the working ability of the dogs of their specific breeds. The American Chesapeake Club calls theirs ''Working Dog Certificate Tests'' but the underlying idea is the same. Appropriate titles (see above) are awarded by the national breed club to dogs which pass the various levels of these tests: WC, WD, WCX, WDX, WDQ. While these titles are not recognized by any registry, they have meaning among the members of the national breed clubs, so have had a significant impact on breeding practices. Specific requirements for each.title can be obtained from the awarding national club.

WORKING RETRIEVER (WR): title awarded by NAHRA to a dog which has earned 20 points in the Intermediate (middle level) stake. The dog earns 5 points for each successful completion, so it takes 4 completions to win the titles. This is comparable to the AKC ''Senior Hunter'' (SH) title. However, NAHRA titles are placed before the dog's name while AKC titles are placed after it.

APPENDIX II

Important Contacts

All-Breed Registries

American Kennel Club (AKC)
    51 Madison Avenue
    New York, NY 10010

United Kennel Club (UKC)
    100 East Kilgore Road
    Kalamazoo, MI 49001-5598

Field Dog Stud Book (FDSB)
    222 West Adams Street
    Chicago, IL 60606

Magazines for Hunting Retriever Owners

GUN DOG
    1901 Bell Avenue, Suite 4
    P.O. Box 35098
    Des Moines, IA 50315

HUNTING RETRIEVER (UKC magazine)
    100 East Kilgore Road
    Kalamazoo, MI 49001-5598

HUNTER'S WHISTLE (AKC magazine)
    51 Madison Avenue
    New York, NY 10010

NAHRA NEWS
    P.O. Box 154
    Swanton, VT 05488

RETRIEVER FIELD TRIAL NEWS
    4213 South Howell Avenue
    Milwaukee, WI 53207

Hunting Test Sponsors

American Kennel Club (AKC)
    51 Madison Avenue
    New York, NY 10010

United Kennel Club (UKC)
    100 East Kilgore Road
    Kalamazoo, MI 49001-5598

North American Hunting Retriever Association (NAHRA)
    P.O. Box 154
    Swanton, VT 05488

National Breed Clubs

American Chesapeake Club
    Carol C. Anderson
    373 Stafford Court
    Lake Forest, IL 60045

American Water Spaniel Club
    Thomas E. Olson
    Route 4, Box 231
    Milaca, MN 56353

Curly-Coated Retriever Club of America
    Sue Tokolics
    303 So. Concord Rd.
    West Chester, PA 19382

Flat-Coated Retriever Society of America
    Gloria Mundell
    829 South Miller Court
    Lakewood, CO 80226

Golden Retriever Club of America
    Bev Brown
    Route 4, Box 4016-B
    Kennewick, WA 99337

Irish Water Spaniel Club of America
 Elissa Kirkegard
 3884 Stump Road
 Doylestown, PA 18901

Labrador Retriever Club, Inc.
 John McAssey
 121 Main Street
 Boise, ID 83702

Nova Scotia Duck Tolling Retriever Club (USA)
 Marile Waterstraat
 63 Blue Ridge Road
 Penfield, NY 14526

Nova Scotia Duck Tolling Retriever Club (Canada)
 Barb Blake
 8 Mac Avenue
 Guelph, Ontario
 Canada N1H 1M9

Professional Retriever Trainers Association (PRTA)

Secretary:
Jane Laman
4670 Harbour Hills Drive
Manhattan, KS 66502

About the Author

James B. Spencer has been raising, training, showing and trialing retrievers for over twenty years, and has worked with pointing dogs for more than a decade. He has judged licensed field trials as well as all three types of hunting retriever tests, and conducted seminars for retriever clubs throughout the country.

An award-winning freelance writer by profession, Spencer is well-known to readers of *Gun Dog, Wildfowl, Retriever International, Hunting Retriever, Dog Fancy, Wing and Shot*, and other periodicals. He also contributes a monthly column on the "Business of Writing" to the Dog Writers Association of America newsletter and serves as one of the judges of their annual writing competition. A member of both DWAA and Outdoor Writers Association of America, Spencer is recognized for the humor and quick wit that laces his writing. **Hunting Retrievers** is his second book; the first, **Retriever Training Tests** was published by Arco in 1983.

A native of the midwest, he is married and the father of five children.

Looking for more information to help you with your dog?

The following titles may be purchased at your local bookstore or pet supply outlet, or ordered direct.

_____ **Retriever Puppy Training: The Right Start for Hunting,** Rutherford and Loveland. $8.98

_____ **Scent—Training to Track, Search, and Rescue,** Pearsall and Verbruggen. $15.98

_____ **Owner's Guide to Better Behavior in Dogs & Cats,** William Campbell. $10.98

_____ **How to Raise a Puppy You Can Live With,** Rutherford and Neil. $7.98

_____ **Canine Hip Dysplasia and Other Orthopedic Diseases,** Lanting. $15.98

_____ **Complete catalog of pet books.**

Include Postage $2.00 first book, 75¢ each additional book. Colorado residents add 3% sales tax. Prices subject to change without notice.

_____ Payment enclosed   Please charge my _____ Visa _____ MasterCard
Card No. _____ Exp. Date _____

Name _____
Address _____
City _____ State _____ Zip _____

Write to:

Alpine Publications, 2456 E. 9th St. #B, Loveland, CO 80537